D1525734

CONSTANTINA SAFILIOS-ROTHSCHILD
is Professor of Sociology
and Director of the Family Research Center
at Wayne State University

LOVE, SEX, AND SEX ROLES

Constantina Safilios-Rothschild

A SPECTRUM BOOK

PRENTICE-HALL, INC.
Englewood Cliffs, New Jersey 07632

Library of Congress Cataloging in Publication Data

SAFILIOS-ROTHSCHILD, CONSTANTINA (date).
   Love, sex, and sex roles.

   (A Spectrum Book)
   Bibliography: p.
   Includes index.
   1. Interpersonal relations.   2. Love.   3. Sex.
4. Sex role.   I. Title.
HQ18.U5S23   301.41   76-44439
ISBN 0-13-540948-9
ISBN 0-13-540930-6 pbk.

A SPECTRUM BOOK

10   9   8   7   6   5

Printed in the United States of America

Prentice-Hall International, Inc., *London*
Prentice-Hall of Australia Pty. Limited, *Sydney*
Prentice-Hall of Canada, Ltd., *Toronto*
Prentice-Hall of India Private Limited, *New Delhi*
Prentice-Hall of Japan, Inc., *Toyko*
Prentice-Hall of Southeast Asia Pte. Ltd., *Singapore*
Whitehall Books Limited, *Wellington, New Zealand*

Contents

Preface   vii

INTRODUCTION   1

One   **LOVE IS A MANY-SPLENDORED THING**   5
Love Is Love Is Love . . .   5
Love and Marriage like Horse and Carriage   16
Love and Sexuality through Masculinity and Femininity   21

Two   **WOMEN AS OBJECTS**   26
The Value of Women   26
Women's Evaluation of Themselves   35

Three **MEN AS OBJECTS:**
THE VENGEANCE OF THE VICTIM 41

Men as Sex Objects *41*
Men as Children *50*

Four **OBSTACLES TO THE DEVELOPMENT OF LOVE** 54

The Dehumanization of Love and Sex *54*
Myths about Love *65*
Is Love Possible between Unequals? *70*

Five **STRANGERS, FRIENDS, AND COLLEAGUES** 80

Encounters with Strangers *82*
Working Together *86*
On Being Friends *94*

Six **THE PERILS OF TRANSITION** 99

New Questions and New Answers *99*
The Performance Trap: Women Must Also Perform *107*
The New Threats to Men *112*

Seven **THE FUTURE FOR LOVE AND SEX** 116

Sex for the Sake of Sex *117*
Women Can Also Pursue *119*
Sex: Beyond Performance *123*
Humanizing Sex and Love *126*
The "Hot" and "Cool" Dilemmas of the Future *128*

References 139

Index 149

Preface

During the last few years a great number of books have been written about different aspects of human sexuality. "How-to" manuals have become bestsellers, and books on sex roles and the psychology of women have become household items. Recently a few authors have started discussing the many profound and difficult dilemmas of sexual relationships and love that are evolving. This book is an effort to analyze sexuality in the context of different relationships as well as in the context of sex roles. The crucial questions about men's or women's sexuality and about love and commitment cannot be answered unless they are seen in terms of the complex dynamics of the interrelationships among sexuality, emotions and love feelings, and masculinity and femininity.

Many of the readers of this book have been socialized for a different emotional world than the one with which they have to cope now. In this respect I represent an extreme, since I was socialized to be a "good" girl in a far more traditional era and society. From my adolescence in Greece to my adulthood in the United States amidst many "liberations" and "sexual revolutions," I have been affected by a tremendous amount of social change and cultural evolution. This background has been quite helpful in my analysis of the traditional underpinnings of sex, love, and gender. In addition, a series of clinical interviews I took from rural and urban low-income, traditional Greek men and women have helped me understand more about what it means to love, to have sexual relations, and to suffer in unloving marriages in such a traditional sex-role context.

Although in the U.S. today we have overcome a number of old hangups, many of our transitional problems can be better understood if they are seen as a stage in the evolution from the traditional past to a vastly different future. I have tried to analyze evolution, starting with the most traditional societies, regions, and subgroups. I chose Southern Europe, the Middle East, and North Afric because I am most familiar with these traditional cultural areas, and recent studies have helped us understand the dynamics of these areas. At present many different types of transitions are going on. The stress is often enormous as men and women undergo profound changes in the way they define themselves and their relationships with others. Sometimes the newly gained rights, freedoms, and options are too much — not all of us are able to take advantage of all those opportunities and possibilities. Some settle for a variety in expressing their sexuality but shy away from love and commitment. Others hang on to the traditional conceptions of "maleness" and "femaleness" and restrict themselves to relationships, roles, and behaviors that do not satisfy them or fulfill them. Still others are flexible enough to change but do not have the skills to evaluate the psychic cost that may be involved; all too often they experiment with unhappy results.

It is important to understand the nature of the transition that we are undergoing and the conflicts and dilemmas that besiege us. We must raise the crucial questions even when we cannot answer them all. That is what I have tried to do, basing my analysis on research studies, impressionistic writing, sociological and anthropological analyses, and experiential data. I hope that every person who reads the book will find his/her own experiences, emotions, feelings, doubts, fears, and delights reflected throughout its pages. For I have tried to present sociological analysis from a perspective that includes the emotional richness of people's real lives and that also reflects my own experiences and dilemmas. Clearly I am restricted by my experiential framework as well as by the focus of the available research so that the discussion of the transitional issues and dilemmas may be more relevant and valid for middle- and upper-middle-class men and women than for others.

While I was writing this book many of my friends, men and women of all ages, read different drafts and discussed them endlessly with me. I want to single out a few who decisively influenced the way I approached issues. Mania Pavela Ribbens, a Greek professor of electrical engineering, and Danny Ribbens, a mathematician and professor of computer science, read very early drafts and struggled along with me while I was thinking out loud. The mathematical mind of Danny Ribbens forced me to a more disciplined thinking and writing style and his clear, critical, incisive comments helped me understand the male point of view. We argued a lot but I never argued more productively. Lynne Dobrofsky, a dear friend and colleague, read early drafts and gave me many insights in emerging trends in love and sexuality. May Ahdab Yehia, earlier my student at Wayne State University, helped me better understand women's love and sexuality in the Arab countries. Furthermore, Gail Jacob, my assistant, not only helped me express myself better in English but also enriched my insights into the problems and views of the young generation of women. Furthermore, I am most grateful to my colleagues Arlie Hochschild, Jacques Dofny, and Lillian Troll who generously gave me their most precious time and made invaluable critical comments on this book. I especially appreciate Arlie's sharing her first weeks after the birth of her baby with my book! I owe much to the endless discussions with students, friends, and colleagues on life and love; it is these that have made sociological knowledge and insights come alive. Irene Zak, my good friend and trusted secretary, has typed this book with love and dedication. Finally, deepest thanks to Mary Allen, who copyedited it, and to Carol Smith, who oversaw its production, with equal love, skill, and dedication.

INTRODUCTION

Seen in an historical and cross-cultural perspective, love, sexuality, and marriage have seldom been expected to coincide. Each has followed quite independent developments, and it is only in contemporary Western societies that they have been "squeezed" together into one cultural package (Hochschild, 1976). There is nothing "natural" about a close association of love, sexuality, and marriage. People living in different eras and societies have or have not combined them, depending on a number of structural factors such as: the type and level of economy in the society; the prevailing class system and the existing channels for upward social mobility; the degree of social differentiation; and the prevailing notions of masculinity and femininity and the extent of social equality between men and women.

In general, the less differentiated the society—considering the economic and political organization coinciding with the institution of the family—the more separated sexuality, love, and marriage are from one another. The more differentiated the society—and, therefore, the more the economic and political organization (as well as other social institutions such as religion, education, etc.) become separated from the family system—the more likely is marriage to be a private contract rather than an institution and the more love and sexuality will be combined with marriage (Collins, 1975; Hochschild, 1976).

This book focuses on societies that are already differentiated but differ in crucial structural variables. The Arab societies and the traditional segments of the Greek and Italian societies represent examples of societal groups at an early stage of societal differentiation in which there are few avenues for social mobility. Because of this, marriage often represents a chance for social mobility and is, therefore, supposed to be a social and economic arrangement rather than one inspired by love. Only upper- and upper-middle-class men in these societies can choose to combine love and sexuality in their marriages, since they do not depend on their wives for improvement of their social standing in terms of money, social connections, or power and influence.

Because of the striking social inequality between men and women prevailing in these societies and women's inability to have independent access to social standing, sexuality is their only negotiable resource to be exchanged for status. Women's sexuality, therefore, becomes "politicized" (Hochschild, 1976), and they develop a wide range of sexual strategies and intrigues to maximize their bargaining power* One such strategy involves the kind of sexual repression that makes sexuality a "scarce good," the value of which becomes in this way artificially increased. The notion of femininity plays a very important role in the politicization of women's sexuality by justifying women's sexual repression and passivity on a "natural," biological basis. This notion makes it possible for women to be admired when they can make themselves sexually attractive, while idealizing and only hinting at the sexuality that is withheld and exchanged (Collins, 1975).

---

*The only exception to this has been high-status women, who because of their inherited wealth, prestige, and power could bargain from a privileged position almost on a par with men. Like high-status men, they have had the option of combining love and sexuality in marriage.

Thus women become experts in sexual teasing, learning how to use sex as a commodity, and come to be viewed and view themselves as sex objects (see Chapters 2, 3, and 4). Also, the notion of romantic love further justifies and adds to women's sexual repression (Collins, 1975) and convinces men to make long-term economic and social commitments to women through marriage in exchange for their sexuality.

It is the central thesis of this book that when men and women are drastically unequal and women occupy a clearly inferior, disadvantaged sociological position, they necessarily become psychologically unequal; then men and women are unable to understand each other and to relate to each other as human beings. Instead they tend to use each other as objects and try to "win" in the game of exchanging sexuality for commitment and security, sometimes referred to as the "battle of the sexes." Within this context, the development of a mature, fulfilling love has been almost impossible, and whenever it has happened, it has represented nothing short of a miracle! As we shall see, this has led not only to the separation of love from marriage but also to the separation of love from sexuality and to a profound alienation of men and women from their feelings and emotions.

As long as sex-role stereotypes and discrimination make it impossible for most women to improve themselves, a curious phenomenon exists: only men can, if they choose, marry the women they love. As long as most women still must depend on their husbands for income, economic security, and social status, they cannot afford to rely primarily on love as the basis for marriage. They must marry men who can guarantee them social status and a satisfactory standard of living.* Because, however, love is idealized without notable exception for women, as we shall see in greater detail in Chapter 1, women become "love experts" who learn how to define, manipulate, direct, and redefine their feelings and emotions so as to keep at least the illusion of love.

---

*Upper-class women have the privileged option of marrying the man they love regardless of his economic and status achievements. This option is, however, rarely exercised outside the class confines primarily because marriage in this class involves the transfer of great wealth, which is family-based, and, thus, marriage remains more of a "clan" affair than an individual contract.

As women are increasingly able to find work more easily, even if to be paid low wages and salaries, they are able to partially depoliticize their sexuality, a process considerably aided by the development of birth control methods and the increasing separation of sexuality from reproduction. But it is only in the last decade that the women's liberation movement and ideology have brought about significant social changes in the North American and Scandinavian societies and to some extent also in some Western European societies—changes that slowly but consistently lead toward social and economic equality between men and women.

This increasing equality opens up the possibility for the complete depoliticization of sexuality and love and allows speculation about the evolution of all types of intimate relationships. Women's increasing economic independence from men for the first time frees love from economic considerations. Men and women may be free to choose to love another human being without the traditional overriding concerns for social status, income, or power. It will become less and less necessary to compromise the possibility of experiencing love by using sexuality and emotions as resources. Other characteristics—such as mutual attractiveness, understanding, tenderness, sexual compatibility, and a variety of interpersonal skills—can become salient elements in the choice of a love partner. Societal pressure to establish traditional marriage and family patterns as symbols of maturity, normality, and social responsibility will lessen. Marriage, sexuality, and love, even when combined, will no longer necessarily imply lifelong commitments.

As love, sexuality, and marriage increasingly become free options for people rather than instruments in the pursuit of security, women and men may discover that they can relate to, like, and love each other as human beings rather than as objects and in many different types of intimate relationships. Love can become a mature and fulfilling way of expressing one's own humanity. It is with the hope of hastening this process that this book is offered.

One

LOVE IS
A MANY – SPLENDORED THING

Love is Love is Love . . .

It has often been claimed that love is so subjective and so elusive that it defies definition—there are almost as many ways to love as there are people. There is no doubt that the expressions of love vary from culture to culture, era to era, and person to person. In some periods "real" love had to be romantic and free of the "ugliness" of sex. In other times sexual expression was considered the most vital ingredient of love. For many years and in many societies, love has meant emotional and sexual exclusivity. Most recently love has meant being "cool" by letting people be themselves.

The variety of love is further complicated and amplified by the fact that each person may express love very differently toward different people and during different stages of life. The same person may be jealous and possessive in one love relationship and flexible and open in another. Two lovers who separate and reunite after some years may love each other very differently the second time around. Maturity often brings about different expressions of love, sometimes with fewer emotional highs and lows but with more understanding and tenderness.

Because of this considerable variability, no single definition of love has ever been satisfactory. There are, however, some elements which, although they vary in degree and intensity, have to be present in a valid love relationship. They include: (a) the willingness to please and accommodate the other even if this entails compromises or sacrifices;* (b) the acceptance of the other for what (s)he is, including faults and shortcomings; and (c) as much concern about the loved one's welfare as about one's own. Clearly, these elements are ideal, but when they are not present to any degree and intensity, the relationship is apt to be more of an exploitative nature, or one involving "limited responsibility." In a recent family research study in Detroit, a man described what he thought of as the behavior of a loving husband:

> Her contentment and happiness are more important to him than anything else. He gives her the kind of attention that would make him aware of her needs and interests. He admires and respects her. There is a warmth of feeling between them that shows.

According to the degree and intensity with which the above elements are present in a love relationship and according to the extent to which additional elements such as total identification of the one with the other, sexual attraction, passion, playfulness, friendships, etc. are present, one could distinguish different types of love relationships: "love-adventure," "amitié amoureuse"

*A recent analysis of love has gone even further. Judith Milstein Katz says that in order for a behavior to be considered as love: (a) the behavior must be initiated by the person in love (the loved one "does not have to ask"); (b) it must be well-timed in that the desirable behavior takes place when the loved one desires it most; and (c) the behavior must represent some kind of sacrifice for the loving person. In this sense the loving person must be able to guess (rather than be told) what the loved person likes and when he (she) likes it and offer it, especially when this desirable behavior requires some effort, time, money, or other cost (Katz, 1976).

(love-friendship), passionate love, affectionate love, and "mature" love. These types are of course "ideal." No love relationship can be neatly categorized. Each relationship has a variety of elements and it may be frequently transformed from one type to another (Kilpatrick, 1975).

The "love-adventure" variety is oriented toward fun and games, pleasure and enjoyment, and it usually involves little commitment and responsibility. This is well-represented in the "cool" love relationships presently admired in our society. Men and women may have several such love-adventures simultaneously or intermittently without one affecting the other (at least, this is what is believed). Or, love-adventure may provide spice and variety while an affectionate love within the context of marriage provides tenderness, continuity, and meaning.

At this point it should be clarified that when one becomes involved in some kind of an emotional alliance, he or she can seldom regulate and control the type of relationship that may eventually evolve. One may feel like having a "fun-and-games" adventure and end up being passionately in love. It is difficult to "bargain" for a specific type of love relationship; most often its unfolding bursts with surprises.

The love-friendship variety does not usually involve sex and is sometimes the type of love relationship that remains after a passionate love has run its course. In some cases, love-friendship may resemble considerably the "affectionate love" type in terms of the existing concern and interest and even the sacrifices made for the other. This is particularly true when the love-friendship follows a passionate love, because the man and woman involved have shared many experiences. Love-friendship does not usually have possessive and exclusive elements. The two people involved feel free to be themselves, and to have other types of love relationships. Their special bond provides them with tender reassurance and support. There is, however, the potential for this love-friendship to be transformed into affectionate love; it can even become a type of passionate love that has the power to transform the most drab life, to make the most unhappy circumstances tolerable and even sweet. Here the Persian proverb applies: "When you walk hand in hand with your lover even hell becomes paradise." Passion has, however, a negative and torturous side. Because of the intensity of the feelings, the slightest negligence, indifference, or disappointment can provoke great unhappiness. One gives everything (or believes so) but also expects everything in return, making the contract quite difficult to fulfill at all times. Passionate love makes one totally emotionally vulnerable, and only when this openness and vulnerability are reciprocal is the relationship possible. When the one partially controls feelings and puts up defenses the other is automatically hurt (Firestone, 1970); at least until the more vulnerable one is also able to shift to a lower gear and by this process achieve a less intense relationship. Passions can be frustrating, disappointing, and exhausting. Conflicts and quarrels often go hand in hand with passionate love because expectations are high; seldom does the other person love you according to your rules of loving. Unless they are too frequent and unreasonable, however, these conflicts tend to intensify the love feelings rather than to weaken them.

Many people are afraid of passions not only because of the loss of control involved but also because passions are volatile and unstable. Passionate loves can go flat, or can die as violently and abruptly and inexplicably as they start. Loss of passion can bring deadly loneliness, emptiness, and despair, especially when the end has been sudden. The agony felt by the deserted lover is deep and the wounds painful. Frequently the reaction to this hurt is numbness, inability to feel anything for a long time. It is this pain that so many people dread. But even so, it is difficult not to long for and dream of the excitement and intensity of a passionate love.

"Passionate" love bears some similarities to what has often been called "romantic" love. In a research study conducted in Holland, respondents characterized "true" love in these terms: (a) you meet your true love only once in a lifetime; (b) if you love someone, this person becomes the only purpose in your life;* (c) both persons involved sense true love immediately; (d) true love leads to an almost perfect happiness; and (e) true love is eternal (Kooy, 1969). It is important to note further that many people in Holland and the U.S. (as well as other Western nations) still believe at least to some extent in this notion of love. Young women, more than young men, still tend to hold to the ideal of romantic love, probably because they continue to be pro-grammed for it by their upbringing. The fact that they usually fall in love many times before (and/or after) they marry can always be explained; these episodes are not "true" love. Or whenever a love does not lead to happiness, it is said to be because it is not "true" love. Thus, one may eternally seek "true" love (Benson, 1971; Bell, 1971).

The notion of romantic love has its basis in the past. Men and women most often loved only once in their lives partly because their life expectancy was much shorter and partly because in most cases their lifestyle did not allow them to meet a great variety of people. It was not uncommon for those who had gone once through the trials and tribulations of a great love to deliberately dull their feelings, control their emotions, and refuse to fall in love again. Now, however, in most developed societies people may often become attracted to and fall in love with several others (Bell, 1976). This occurs not only because they meet many people, but also because they have been conditioned to believe that love is a necessary ingredient in life. Without love, they have been told time after time, life is a burden and a bore and it is questionable whether it is worth all the trouble.

This extension of the opportunity to love also extends the opportunity to feel pain and disappointment as well as pleasure and excitement. The possibility of loving many people throughout a long life may be responsible for the redefinition of love that is taking place today. This redefinition is quite radical,

*According to this definition very few Western, middle- and upper-middle-class men, predominately preoccupied with work and achievement, ever expressed "true" love.

for it presents the view that love relationships are not necessarily eternal even when they are quite strong. If people can accept that probably they will love intensely several times during their lifetime, they may learn to approach love, separation, commitment, marriage, and divorce with a healthier outlook. The end of love (for both or for one) may be less shattering and disorganizing if people can look forward to other loves. Perhaps people can learn to love while maintaining their personality and identity as a continuing link from one love to another. The early realization that there is no such thing as "one true love" may make it easier to be more tolerant, more understanding, and more open toward those they love.

Sometimes romantic passion slowly diminishes in strength and becomes transformed into a stable and tender "affectionate love" that is able to withstand the responsibilities, problems, routine, and even boredom that come with a lasting relationship. Affectionate love may involve different mixes of sexual attraction, friendship, intellectual exchanges, understanding, tenderness, and concern for the welfare as well as for the soul of the other. But usually none of these elements is in excess. There is a blend that pleases, reassures, comforts, and has a good chance of lasting. The high peaks and deep valleys disappear; in their place is constancy and predictability. In addition, there is an important characteristic that distinguishes this type of love from romantic love, which is self-centered love in that one is "more in love with the feeling of love than with the beloved" (Kilpatrick, 1975). In affectionate love the other person is accepted as a person in his/her own right. That is why the affectionate rather than the romantic type of love is usually compatible with marriage.

"Mature" love is probably very rare because not too many people are skilled enough to work toward its accomplishment. In order to achieve this type of love, one has to make great efforts; mature love is "more under the control of will . . . and less under the control of emotions . . . ." (Kilpatrick, 1975). Because they may have become socialized to play destructive power games with others, even in love, many people do not achieve mature love.

Others are awkward and simply do not know how to maintain stability and strength in the love relationship. Ingmar Bergman, the Swedish movie director, has correctly said, "When it comes to feelings, we are all illiterate." How many people know how to avoid trying to control the one they love — to let the loved one be free, and yet help that person grow as an individual? How many can be aware of the real needs of the one they love? And how many know how to love deeply without submerging their own unique self? How many can find the perfect equilibrium of depth of feelings, independence, dependence, growth and stability, and fulfillment through their love? And of those who finally manage to achieve this precious balance, how many know how to keep it intact while everything else keeps changing, including themselves?

Whatever the type of love relationship, we know very little about the alchemy of love. What, in fact, makes people "fall" in love? Why is it that one may meet hundreds of people who are pleasant, attractive, and interesting and feel nothing special and then meet a person who suddenly stirs one's soul? Why is it possible to feel empty and deflated in the middle of a pleasant and smooth love adventure and feel fulfilled by and attached to a person in a difficult, conflict-ridden, even joyless relationship? In *Carmen*, a song claims that "love has never known rules." Moreover, the intensity of love is usually unequal. Lovers may start at the same level, but with time one may become more emotionally dependent and make more compromises and sacrifices than the other.

What we do know is that love of all kinds — friendly, passionate, affectionate, and mature — gives meaning to people's lives and diminishes their loneliness. People want to hang on to life because they need and love others and/or because they know that others love and need them. We must clarify here that not only heterosexual (or homosexual) love but also the mother-child or brother-sister love or the love between friends can play a determinative role in a person's life. Knowing that somebody else really cares for us diminishes our feeling of alienation in a confusing and difficult world. Love involves the overlapping of the personal spaces of two people (Firestone, 1970); the one cannot be happy if the other is not happy (Masters and Johnson, 1975). In successful love relationships, each person wants to make the other happy because in this way his or her own happiness increases. Even in less successful, less reciprocal relationships, the feeling of love usually diminishes the existential loneliness and emptiness, unless the psychological cost of love becomes so high that even loneliness becomes a welcome alternative.

Because love gives meaning to our lives and eases our loneliness, it is only natural that often we tend to become psychologically dependent upon the one we love. And the more we love someone, the greater is that inclination. Though this may be natural, the weight of dependency can become heavy on a love relationship and can destroy it. A very delicate balance of dependency and independence is needed for love to flourish. Such a balance may be achieved by spreading dependencies over many possible alternatives in addition to love, such as friendships, work, ideologies, hobbies, as well as objects (a house, a garden, a pet). In this way it is possible to remain essentially ourselves, independent of any single relationship, activity, or object. But can such a careful balance, sought in the desire for a calm, fulfilled, and evenly contented life, make us happy? Are we not all drawn toward one passion that can make us neglect most other interests and ties although we know or suspect the high emotional cost? Sometimes we may consciously and willingly pay the price in order to experience at least once the exhilarating "high" of an exclusive, all-devouring passion.

But still the crucial question is not answered: What makes people fall in love and what sustains love? The alchemy of love still escapes our analysis and understanding. Most people have a vague, amorphous image of the type of person they like and admire and to whom they usually become attracted. Some place a high value on a slim silhouette and an intellectual, idealistic outlook; others need an earthy, sensual, passionate person who is more oriented towards emotions than towards thoughts. But these images usually delimit only the range of people who have the potential of becoming attractive. Still something else is needed, something of vital importance: a spark, a "click," which we do not understand and cannot control. Furthermore, why is it that this crucial "click" happens in one person and not in the other, even when the basic requirements for attraction are met? Probably the most crucial factors on which initial attraction is based are largely irrational and subconscious, and it is only after we are already attracted that we start justifying our attraction on the basis of the characteristics we cherish. Whether or not an initial love attraction will last and develop may depend on a number of factors. Clearly, *love* does not follow the same laws as *liking*. People tend to *like* people who reward them. But people do not necessarily love the one "who provides them the most rewards with the greatest consistency. Passion sometimes develops under conditions that would seem more likely to provoke aggression and hatred than love" (Walster, 1974). In fact, sometimes rejection and indifference may increase the love feelings, and a great number of obstacles often have the same effect (Walster, 1974). Of course, in this case we are talking about passionate or romantic love, in which the focus is more on the love *feelings* than the person involved.

There are some indications that an aura of desirability (even artifically created) tends to attract people. Most people would like to "possess" something valuable and desirable and tend, therefore, to fall in love with people who are already loved or at least desired by others. This seems to be particularly true in the case of men. Experimental research has indicated that a women who is hard-to-get for all other men but easy-to-get for a particular man is preferred to a uniformly hard-to-get or a uniformly easy-to-get woman (Walster et al., 1973). In addition, many men and women are often attracted and challenged by someone who is absorbed by work, an ideal, or some other central preoccupation that gives them meaning and fulfills them as human beings. Up to now men have typically been absorbed in this way, but increasingly women have the same options. Such women do not become dependent on their lovers and are able to play a "cool" game in their relationships with men. And this may make them seem elusive, interesting, and exciting to certain men. A woman who seeks to affirm her own personality and interests rather than totally surrendering herself to a man may bewilder and even threaten some men, but others may find her challenging and desirable because of this.

While we are discussing the role that a woman's dedication to work or to an ideal can play in enhancing her attractiveness or in maintaining a love relationship, it is worthwhile to examine the love experiences of earlier "liberated" women.

Throughout history there have been women who maintained their independence, their personality, and their significant involvement in work, art, or an ideal. Alexandra Kollontai, probably the first "liberated" woman according to present terminology, lived during the early 1900s in Russia.* She analyzed the "new" breed of heroines presented in novels of the postrevolutionary era. Her analysis shows that these women were striking and unique because they struggled to put their identity, growth, self-fulfillment, and scientific or artistic achievements on a level equal to or higher than love and passion. They were portrayed as unmarried women who lived together with the man they loved usually only for a few years. They were often absorbed by their work, their interests, and their ideals; they refused to become the reflection or the shadow of a man and they often ended a passionate love relationship because it interfered with their dedication to work or to ideals.

Actually, some of these "liberated" women behaved in a way that parallels some men's attitudes toward love involvements. They deliberately avoided relationships that they feared might sidetrack them from their life purpose (Stora-Sandor, 1973).

---

*Here it is important to note that the "liberation" of Alexandra Kollontai, initially an important political figure in the Russian revolution, was in fact quite embarrassing and unacceptable to the male-dominated political establishment. These pioneer "liberated" women were not admired, encouraged, or rewarded by the official party line. Kollontai herself was to some extent ostracized and put in the periphery by being sent off to Sweden and Finland as the Russian ambassador.

Like these early "liberated" Russian counterparts, today's career women often face the same dilemmas and experience the same frustrations. And they have the same difficulty subduing their "feminine" tendencies (deeply ingrained through socialization) to surrender themselves entirely to a man. When they fail to do this, it may spell disaster for any love relationship. They may try to possess the man they love, overwhelming him in an attempt to fill the void created by the temporary relinquishment of their other life-absorbing activities and preoccupations.

An interesting question that can be raised here concerns the extent to which a man *or* woman can feel and satisfy two passions—one for work or an ideal and one for a lover. Each passion may demand total commitment and dedication; two may be incompatible, only able to co-exist for brief interludes. One passion tends to take priority over the other. That is why some men have mistrusted passionate love relationships and instead focused their total energies on wars, expeditions, politics, revolutions, research, or writing. This incompatibility has been recognized in Arab cultures, in which a man's passion for a woman was condemned because it implied a lesser religious dedication (Mernissi, 1973 and 1975). Furthermore, we do not know whether the degree of incompatibility increases or decreases when *both* people in a love relationship are also absorbed in work or an ideal. Data from two-career marriages indicate that such a dual dedication on the part of both spouses sometimes enhances rather than interferes with the relationship (Rapoport and Rapoport, 1971).

It may be a sad and bitter conclusion that for some an important element in love seems to be a certain amount of elusiveness and insecurity. The standard that one should never allow total commitment, vulnerability, or unconditional caring and love may indeed be valid for some, but we must ask what are the costs of such an outlook. The costs are also great for those who spend their lives unhappily pursuing impossible and unrealistic loves. What is the best course in the search for personal fulfillment? Maybe only in a "mature" love relationship is it possible for two people to appreciate and enjoy one another's open and total commitment and love. Too many people are frightened of committing themselves to loving one person, of becoming totally open and vulnerable. In this book we will investigate some of the implications of this fear.

Love and Marriage
Like Horse and Carriage

For many centuries in many societies love and marriage have been almost entirely separate and sometimes even diametrically opposed. Until recently and in most cultures, love has been considered entirely separate from marriage and from sex. "Real" love could only be platonic and never consummated and sexuality was not thought of as exclusively confined to marriage. It is reported that in the "love courts" held by the wives of knights in the twelfth century, the conclusion was that real love could not exist in a legitimate marital relationship, because the married man and woman were legally constrained to belong to each other. Real love, they declared, could not exist except when the man and woman could freely and voluntarily commit themselves to one another (Stora-Sandor, 1973).

The idea that love could be a part of marriage began with the development of the middle class in many European countries in the fourteenth and fifteenth centuries. The economic interests of the rising middle class were better served by the existence of a bond of friendship and cooperation and ideally also of love between husbands and wives. Because the accumulation of capital rather than a productive family unit was important to such people, an interested and helpful wife often played a crucial role. Outside the urban middle class, however, because the family represented a productive unit, the foundation of which was primarily utilitarian, love continued to be separated from mar-

riage (Stora-Sandor, 1973). The same has been true for crafts-
men as well as peasants and is still true for urban slum people
and peasants in most of the Third World.

While the ideal of the fusion of love and marriage has
spread primarily to the Western urban middle classes, the
implementation of this ideal varies considerably. In some
societies, such as the U.S., men and women can choose their own
mates freely and love is considered an important factor in a decision to marry. But even in these societies, available research
evidence indicates that other utilitarian factors have been at least
as important as love. In a recent Detroit study, women gave a
multiplicity of reasons for getting married besides love. One
women, for example responded:

> I wasn't madly in love. I was about 31 and I wasn't getting
> any younger. I was getting tired of being by myself and I
> liked him quite a bit. He wouldn't leave me alone. In fact,
> we decided to get married because he spent so much on
> phone bills.

And another woman:

> Financial reasons. It was really rough making ends meet.
> We shared the rent. I also liked him and respected him. He
> says what he thinks, never tells a lie.

Women, of course, because of traditional sex discrimination,
have been socialized to look for men who can assure them of the
desired social status and standard of living; love is apt to be
secondary to this basic condition. Because women have had to
"screen" men in terms of their actual and potential social status,
they appeared to be less spontaneous than men. After this initial
screening process is successfully completed, women allow
themselves to experience the emotional, idealized, romantic love
components more intensely than men. Men have been found to
fall in love more readily and spontaneously earlier in the relationship than women (Kanin et al., 1970), probably because

their love feelings are developed primarily on the basis of the woman's feminine qualities—her attractiveness and "nice" personality (sweetness, gentleness, pliability). Many studies have shown that men rank attractiveness much higher than women (Combs and Kenkel, 1966; Kephart, 1967), since men give their social status to the women they marry and can therefore be less concerned with this issue. In the author's recent Detroit study men, much more often than women, answered that they had married because they loved their wives or because she was "right" for them in terms of attractiveness and personality ("She was attractive, intelligent, and witty"). Some men, however, mentioned reasons other than love, such as: "I was ready to settle down. I felt I had played around long enough." So in a sense they found themselves in a psychological moment at which they were prepared to link love with marriage.

In many Third-World nations, the ideal of the fusion of love and marriage is interpreted and implemented quite differently. The notion exists that it is important for marriage to be based on social (and to some extent also on psychological) compatibility out of which love may grow slowly as the spouses share the joys, sorrows, and responsibilities of married life. To some extent, this interpretation represents an adaptation to the realities of life, which obliges people to pay more attention to economic and social considerations than to feelings when planning a marriage that usually represents a lifelong commitment. In many of these societies, the percentage of single men and women is quite high; this is still true for such countries as Japan, Greece, Tunisia, and the Central and South American nations. The reasons are many; in Greece, for instance, the notion has developed that "marriage kills love," and thus marriage is not seen as the "natural" culmination of love.

The emergence of the idea that love is destroyed by marriage is an important one to consider. First we should clarify what type of love is implied in this notion and then examine the social and economic rationales underlying it.

Most people, when they say that marriage kills love, are

referring to a passionate love in which the one lives for the other, the desires are intense, and the need to express love is continuous. They argue that the necessary routine of marriage, the "availability" of the one to the other, and the emerging difficulties, conflicts, and responsibilities of shared living dilute the passion of love and eventually kill it. But the fact that the passion is lessened or even gone does not necessarily mean that love is dead. It may be simply transformed into affectionate love, or, if the partners are willing to work hard at it, it can become a mature and fulfilling love. The fear in most people's hearts may be that once passion is dead, even if there is still affection, one partner may fall passionately in love with another person. Once a person has experienced a passionate love, the void created by its loss is great, and the longing to experience similar feelings again can propel an individual toward another similar strong emotional attachment.

Beyond these purely emotional fears and considerations, there are also a number of practical, social, and economic motives that make some people fear that love is destroyed by marriage. They judge, and they may be partially correct in this, that love may cloud a person's ability clearly to evaluate the wisdom of entering into a marriage. Under the "spell" of an absorbing and impassioned love relationship, it is reasoned, women and men may lose the ability to assess psychological and social compatibility and measure economic considerations. It is interesting to note that in many developing nations, including Southern Europe, marrying for love is considered a luxury and a privilege of the rich. This has again an economic rationale; social and economic problems and complications are of less concern in the upper classes and, thus, the chances for maintaining love (if not passion) is thought by some to be better.

Regardless of the beliefs concerning the advisability of mixing love and marriage, many people (more than 50 percent in the United States), as we have seen, marry for reasons other than love, ranging from loneliness, desire for marital status, desire for children, financial security, and so on. Another related factor in the belief that love and marriage may *not* go together is the separation in many traditional societies and groups of sexuality from love and/or from marriage. In Italy, for example, and particularly in Central and Southern Italy, men often love women with whom they cannot have sexual relations before marriage. They may in fact stop loving a woman if she agrees to have sexual relations as an expression of love, believing that she is "loose" and thus not worthy of love. Or a man may marry a woman he loves but fulfill his sexuality primarily with a mistress or with prostitutes (Parca, 1968). Even in "developed" societies sexual love may be separated from marriage and/or in nearly half of all marriages there are serious sexual problems and incompatibilities (Lyons, 1972). Furthermore, many men and women increasingly have the opportunity for sexual expression in a variety of casual or less casual relationships (Bell, 1976).

It is true that the attempt to integrate love and sexuality within the marital relationship involves many serious problems, especially if it is believed that one should have sex only with the one he/she loves. Is a divorce the next step when passionate love cools and/or another person becomes the object of sexual love? (see Israel and Eliasson, 1971).* In many Western societies people are increasingly getting divorced when they fail to integrate love and sex in their marriage or become involved in extramarital relationships. Because of these complications, people tend to be skeptical about the long-term survival changes of a love or a satisfactory sexual relationship (whether marital or not). They sadly state that only short-lived relationships unclouded by marital responsibilities can keep their novelty, freshness, and spontaneity. Starting with such a defeatist attitude, they may become easily discouraged *before* they have sought for new and deeper levels of feelings, emotions, and sexual expression. More and more people fail to cope with the letdown that occurs when

---

*Most of us have been socialized to believe that love is a zero-sum game. People are assumed to have a limited, finite quantity of love to give. When one *truly* loves somebody, (s)he is supposed to use *all* this quantity of love. If he or she starts loving someone else it is automatically assumed that the first person is loved less or not at all (Chafetz, 1974).

the original passion is gone; they do not know how to deal with the different phases through which love and sexuality may pass.

Much of the difficulty in modern marriage is the result of the failure to redefine the institution itself in the light of the fairly contemporary idea that love and marriage *do* go together. Today the structure of marriage has changed drastically. The support (as well as the strains) of the extended family has either entirely disappeared or declined. Marriage partners often have to lean almost exclusively on one another. And increasing life expectancy means that we can look forward to (or dread) fifty or sixty married years. What we need is a redefinition of both love and marriage. We need to face the fact that neither may last forever; that potentially they may take place several times in a lifespan. By doing this we do not have to diminish our commitment to the marital relationship. We will only relax our levels of expectation. It is conceivable that such a redefinition of marriage as a possible multiple rather than a unique life event might help us enjoy a marriage as long as it lasts and not necessarily view it or ourselves as a failure when it ends.

Love and Sexuality through Masculinity and Femininity

In trying to understand the independent and interdependent developments of the notions of love and sexuality, it is necessary to acknowledge the evolution of certain structural factors that have affected men's and women's ability to experience and combine love and sexuality. As discussed in the Introduction, these include the kind and level of economy that exist within the context of the particular society; the prevailing class system and the channels that exist for upward social mobility; the degree of social differentiation (i.e., the level of integration of integration of economic, political, religious, educational, etc. institutions with the institution of family and marriage); and the extent of social and economic equality between women and men. Here and in the following chapters we will examine how the stereotypic definitions of masculinity and femininity, resulting from and justifying the present inequality between men and women, have affected their ability to love, express themselves sexually, and integrate love with sexuality.

Sex-role stereotypes have defined men's and women's interest and involvement in love and sex in diametrically opposed directions. In fact, sex has been labeled a "masculine" pursuit and love a "feminine" pursuit. Because of these labels, men have learned to control and dominate sexual relations and to mistrust and avoid love, a foreign territory. They have learned to view love as a "feminine" trick designed to get them to commit themselves to complicated and restraining responsibilities (Safilios-Rothschild, 1975). According to sex-role stereotypes, men are supposed to be afraid and often unable to love and commit themselves. They tend to mistake sex for love; they are mostly interested in sex; when they do "surrender" to love they tend to overromanticize and idealize the woman out of proportion — and once sure of a woman's love, they are apt to lose interest (Firestone, 1970). According to masculine stereotypes, once in love, men are viewed as having "lost" the game and capitulated to the victorious woman. In addition to perpetuating the idea that men should be careful to avoid becoming emotionally involved, even after such an involvement has taken place, masculine stereotypes have encouraged men to struggle to control their feelings and emotions, and resist expressing or even acknowledging them. Such emotional control has been praised and admired as an indication of masculine strength and rationality. In fact, as long as men are able to thus conceal their love feelings, they can still claim their independence and avoid the obligation of making any kind of commitment. Men's stereotypic inability to express their feelings and their awkwardness in love matters has served a very important function: it has itself helped them better control their emotions and resist for as long as possible capitulating to love and the social commitments usually attached to it.

Women, on the other hand, according to the traditional notions of femininity, have been socialized into wanting to fall in love and to capitalize on love feelings. Because their sensitive, emotional, and nurturing character is supposed to be compatible with love, women are seen as being more inclined to love, more faithful, possessive, and dependent on the man. They value romance and affection more than sex, which seems to be the monopoly of traditional masculine men (Firestone, 1970). This sets the stage for the antithesis, the war between the sexes. Men have interest in sex and gain sexual skills and knowledge. Women become the love experts.

Hochschild's (1975) recent research shows that women "work" more on their feelings by analyzing them more as well as by shaping, managing, and directing them more than men. Men, having made the supreme masculine effort to *control* their emotions, can in a sense then afford to let their emotions take over and dictate their choice of sexual and marital partners. Women can allow themselves to be overwhelmed by their emotions — but only when the social conditions surrounding these feelings are "right." When the object of their feelings is not socially acceptable, they "work" on "falling out of love" — they see love as a valuable resource that cannot be wasted without the appropriate social and economic returns. In other words, while and because women have not been socialized traditionally to become skilled in the economic and occupational spheres, they have been allowed to develop skills in the emotional sphere, especially in love (Hochschild, 1975). These skills have not only safeguarded women from falling in love with the "wrong" man but have also allowed them to make believe that they love the man who possesses the desirable social and economic characteristics for marriage. In this way, women maintain the appearance of combining love with sexuality by means of a profoundly alienating process of emotional manipulation.

Up to now, sexuality and love have been the sole trump

cards in women's hands—their passport for making it in the world. Men's fears have therefore been justified, because it is only through love that they are vulnerable. Thus it is understandable that women and men are caught in painful and often tragic dilemmas between their love feelings and needs for sexual expression on the one hand and their desire to conform to the rules and codes concerning the appropriate behavior for men and women on the other.

Parca's study (1968) provides us with interesting insights regarding the changes men undergo as a result of love in a cultural environment in which traditional codes rarely operate, but where "liberation" is nevertheless a difficult achievement. Some North Italian men can reject the ideal of virginity and can even reach the point of preferring to marry a nonvirgin, because they feel that the woman's sexual experiences has matured her and enabled her to better love and better determine whom she wants to marry. Even these men, however, cannot overcome their tendency to evaluate the nature of sexual experiences that women have had; they cannot accept that women may have casual relationships as they have had themselves. That is, love has to justify sexuality in the case of women. It seems that these "transitional" men cease viewing women as objects but in spite of this they cannot accept them as human beings similar to themselves. A few of them can, however, admit that their feelings and emotions are very important to them and that they are emotionally and sexually dependent on a mistress or wife, which is a significant break from traditional masculinity and an important step forward.

In the chapters that follow we will examine in greater detail the implications of socially imposed ideas of masculinity and femininity. In Chapter 2, we will see how the traditional definitions of masculinity and femininity and the implied inferiority of women are ideas that have led to the objectification of women in terms of their only valuable resource: their sexuality. In Chapter 3, we will take a look at how this reduction of women to sex objects, as well as the traditional notions of masculinity, have led in turn to the objectification of men as "sex machines," as children to be manipulated by women. Men and women are socialized to interact with each other as objects at the sexual level rather than as human beings who can relate with, like, and love each other in many different ways. In Chapter 4, we will discuss how the traditional ideas of femininity and masculinity have been incompatible with love, as well as with an open and "human" expression of sexuality for both men and women. This alienating reduction of women-men relationships to sexual objects has not only strained and created problems in friendships and work relationships, as we will see in Chapter 5, but has also deprived love of its mature, fulfilling attributes. In Chapter 6 we will examine the effects of transitional sex-role definitions of love, sexuality, and marriage. And in Chapter 7, on the basis of emerging trends, we will speculate about the future of sex and love—a future in which "liberated" men and women will be able to overcome the idea that there are rigid "masculine" and "feminine" feelings, emotions, thoughts, characteristics, and behaviors and will be able to define themselves similarly as human beings.

Two

WOMEN AS OBJECTS

The Value of Women

Women have always shared many characteristics with perishable, semi-valuable objects. Seldom have they been valued as human beings—for their personalities, feelings, thoughts, or talents; their worth has fluctuated according to properties more characteristic of objects than of people. In traditional societies, the situation is more extreme in that women have been and still are considered quite openly as objects to be traded, exchanged, used, and disposed of when of no further use. In transitional societies in which a variety of social changes are in the process of breaking down some aspects of overt sex discrimination, the processes have become somewhat more subtle and less widespread in all aspects of everyday life. But nevertheless, they are still there.

Objects are usually more valuable and desirable when they are new, unused, beautiful, and/or useful. As we shall see, women have long been judged by these very qualities. A number of important consequences that have greatly affected their options and lives have resulted from this view of women's object-like nature.

Throughout history, young women have been valued more than older women. Despite the fact that age and experience are supposed to mature and enrich men, women have had nothing to gain from age except wrinkles, white hair, and loose flesh. Similarly, women without any type of sexual experience have been given a much higher value than sexually experienced women. (Men, on the other hand, tend to gain considerable value from sexual experience. In fact, those with no sexual experience have been devalued and ridiculed.) Again, as with perishable objects, women have gained nothing positive from "use"; on the contrary, their value diminished. In traditional societies the consequences of the loss of virginity were often inhuman; a father and brother, considering themselves dishonored by such a total devaluation, have had the right to take the woman's life (Safilios-Rothschild, 1972; Paleologos, 1975). Raped and divorced women were (and are) equally devalued. The recent situation in Bangladesh vividly illustrated this when men refused to marry single women raped by Pakistani soldiers and husbands did not want to take back their violated wives. Still at present in some societies in which the loss of virginity removes women from the marriage market, some accommodations have developed allowing women to enjoy premarital sex without being deprived of the option to marry. An ingenious accommodation is a special operation in which their hymen is sewn up again to make them appear virginal for their first wedding night. This operation is widely practiced in several Latin American, Mediterranean, Middle Eastern, and North African societies and is usually resorted to by urban middle- and upper-class women who can afford it (Safilios-Rothschild, 1972; Bradley, 1968).

Objects have no intrinsic value. Their value usually rests on their beauty or usefulness. So women's value has traditionally depended upon their "newness," their attractiveness, and their ability and willingness to serve men. A combination of these is still desirable, although the choice of a wife, as we saw in Chapter 1, is apt to be primarily determined by a woman's looks.* A man who is successful in acquiring a beautiful wife still gains social acceptance, prestige, and admiration.

It is easy to see that this situation has always caused a tremendous amount of anxiety in women. They must continually compare their attractiveness to that of other women-objects around them. The presence of other women (especially if they are unattached and attractive) causes tension and conflict. There is a constant fear that their own value will diminish—their husbands or lovers might decide to "trade them in" for a new, better-looking model. This largely accounts for some women's inability to relax, enjoy, and be friends with other attractive women.

In addition to attractiveness, women's skills as cooks and housekeepers have traditionally been major "selling points." When possible, men have preferred to have a beautiful woman who was willing to serve them, but if this combination has been unavailable, many men settled for a pleasant, accommodating woman who could serve them well. So youth, beauty, and functionality have been the prime qualities in acquiring this very important possession—a wife.

Some types of objects are desired not because of their intrinsic value but because they are admired and desired by many people, especially by important and powerful people. Women have long been in this category of objects. Their worth has been defined in terms of the men who desired them and later on, in terms of the men who acquired them. Even today men† prefer a woman who is sought by many other men; her conquest is a great

---

*In traditional societies, a woman's ability to bear children and particularly sons was (and is) considered very important. This ability was sometimes judged by the number of brothers she had!

†Throughout this chapter the discussed trends and behaviors hold true for most men. There are always some men who do not view women as sex objects, who do not find a woman desirable because other men do, and so on. When the expression "men" is used, the reader should remember that this generalization makes room for some men who are different.

challenge. The high demand for her enhances their victory. Because of this, women learn to emphasize their desirability by creating the illusion that many men want them. Regardless of now beautiful they are, this "high demand" game raises their value and renders them rare and precious things to be possessed by the lucky man. Women who cannot or do not want to play this market game have been and are seen as less desirable and less sought by men.

The fact that a woman's worth is still measured in terms of the man who "owns" her is well illustrated by evidence concerning sentences given to rapists. Longer sentences are given for the rape of married women than for the rape of unmarried or divorced women (Jones and Aronson, 1973; Harrell and Sagan, 1974). It seems that rape is a more serious crime when a man's "possession" is molested, despite the fact that women in both cases are similarly injured. The implication is that a woman who does not belong to a man has no great intrinsic value.

Because women are viewed as objects, men relate to them as to objects and their actions, options, and lives are restricted by rules and limitations applicable to objects. Too many men are preoccupied with the accumulation of many sexual conquests rather than with the development of a warm and deep love relationship with another human being (Israel and Eliasson, 1971). Sexual possession of a woman marks man's ownership. After a man has put his sexual "stamp" of ownership on a woman, he can discard her and add her to his trophies. He has possessed a woman-object that was not precious enough to warrant the effort to keep for life but was sufficiently valuable for the sexual pleasure and sense of domination with which she provided him temporarily. This is exemplified by the men who boast about the fact that they have "had" between 1,000 and 1,200 women (Held, 1975). One can hardly boast of having used so many shirts or shoes! How else could a man "have" so many women except by reducing them to objects, or sexual toys, and by denying that they have any characteristic other than breasts, legs, and genitals?

Men's view of women as objects has been often refined by an evaluation of women as "good" and "bad."* This distinction has been and is much more clear-cut in traditional societies. But its influence is still felt in all societies and even among supposedly "liberated" men. The women in the "good" category have been treated as precious and perishable objects to be protected and cared for, but not touched, enjoyed, or even used. By these terms, "good" women have been obliged to live a very sheltered and restricted life, to experience little, to suffocate without the possibility of self-discovery and growth, and often to be forever denied a good sexual relationship. Within traditional settings, men who love "good" women never have sexual relations with them before marriage. After marriage, sex is mainly for procreation; women seldom have the opportunity to enjoy themselves sexually. This is partly because their image does not allow them to express their sexual needs and partly because their husbands do not expect any great sexual satisfaction from their wives. Husbands in traditional contexts often separate sexual satisfaction from marriage and seek it with "bad" women (Parca, 1968). Thus, good women are left on a shelf like beautiful unused china and are deprived of many experiences and human satisfactions. "Bad" women, on the other hand, are free to experience life. The price for their freedom is high, though; men do not want to own them (at least officially through marriage) and want only to use them for their pleasure and then discard them. Occasionally some "bad" women, even in traditional societies, have, by cleverly using their sexuality, made men want to possess them and support them, even if they did not (or could not) pay the "right price" through marriage.

This whole rationale of "good" and "bad" women has created a cruel dilemma for many women, who have been forced to choose between making themselves "precious" in order to have

---

*In traditional societies, all women are viewed as "bad," since they are seen as objects of temptation and cannot control themselves sexually (Mernissi, 1973). This is why women must be protected and restricted by fathers, brothers, husbands, and sons—they are ideally kept far from men so that they can remain pure and "good."

access to marriage and respectability (while cutting themselves off from many desirable and enjoyable life experiences) or "cheapening" themselves in order to taste life while destroying or jeopardizing their chances for marriage. Either way they remained objects.

One of the consequences of the objectification of women has been that women are not supposed to have opinions, wishes, plans, and an autonomous intelligence. The demonstration of intelligence in a woman was often a surprise to men. And intelligence plus attractiveness comes as a shock because it causes men seriously to question the validity of the "sex-object" image (Stannard, 1971). Intelligence in unattractive women has been usually better tolerated and occasionally even encouraged. Such women have traditionally been seen as having to compensate for their lack of beauty and as having to develop and use their brains to support themselves since the chances that a man would want to "acquire" them and support them were not very good.

Because intelligence and a distinct or strong personality have always been incompatible with the sex-object image of women, they have been advised to hide or play down their intelligence and discouraged from forming strong opinions and preferences. This is supposed to improve their chances of being selected by men as desirable objects to acquire and keep. The idea has been for the husband to mold his wife, a passive object, according to his own image, wishes, and personality so that in fact she would become what he wanted her to be: an extension, or a reflection, of him. In the past wives have internalized their husbands' wishes, preferences, and opinions so that even when they decided or acted for themselves, it was actually as their husbands wanted them to behave.

Because women have been viewed as *passive* objects, incapable of acting independently and determining their own fates, they have been expected to wait to be chosen. Occasionally they can manipulate their circumstances and the man's feelings in order to be chosen by the man they want. But there has been a taboo against directly, openly, and actively choosing a man.

Similarly, once chosen by a man as a lover or a wife, they have been forbidden to initiate sex. Only recently has a more active element been added to the sexual image of women—probably because men have come to feel that in this way women's sexual value as objects is considerably increased.

Women's inability to determine their own lives has been underlined not only by custom by also by law in many developing as well as developed societies. Even in this country women in the very recent past needed a husband's signature and consent to travel abroad, to own property, to borrow money, or even to work. In some traditional societies, women have not been able even to move around freely without being accompanied by a man who in some way "owned" them and protected them. At the present time in Saudi Arabia, a woman cannot enter a cab alone; she must be accompanied by her husband, brother, son or another male relative. Even a 10-year-old son can symbolically "protect" his mother. Furthermore, women have been allowed to move only within a few limited territories defined as "feminine," and in Islamic societies they have for the most part been confined to the home. These spatial constraints have dehumanized women and made them dependent on men. The necessity of having a male escort in order to have access to many territories and be involved in many activities underlines the object-like status of women and makes men's control over women not only inescapable but almost "natural." In our transitional, developed societies women can theoretically go everywhere they want by themselves. The fear of rape, however, significantly controls some women and diminishes their freedom of movement.

Another serious consequence of women's objectification has been their inability to control their own bodies. This lack of control has a tremendous range. Several studies have shown that men touch women much more than women do men (Henley, 1970, 1973). This one-sided touching symbolically shows men's power over women; they feel as free to touch them as they feel free to touch other objects. Touching becomes even more acceptable and institutionalized when women capitalize on their sex-object attributes as strippers, call girls, etc. The extreme of women's lack of control over their own bodies is found in their lack of power in the decision of whether or not to have a child. Husbands and male doctors and legislators have most often decided such things as birth control methods and the availability of abortion. Even when abortion becomes legal in a society, the husband's permission or consent is often necessary and in many societies, a panel of doctors (often predominantly male) can grant the permission for a legal abortion. Furthermore, some recent evidence from the U.S. concerning hysterectomies indicates a very disturbing attitude on the part of male doctors. Some American gynecologists believe that the womb and its accompanying organs are "useless" after childbearing and they are better taken out to avoid cancer! The woman is clearly seen as a childbearing "object" whose parts become obsolete after they have served their purpose. Some doctors go so far as to claim that "women do not mourn the loss of their reproductive organs and capacity the way a man might" (Rodgers, 1975). The most disturbing finding is that because of these attitudes thousands of unnecessary surgical operations take place every year. The available statistics indicate that the large majority of these operations have not been warranted; Rodgers estimates that only 20 percent of them are directly related to cancer or other life-threatening conditions. Other statistics indicate that the post-operative diagnosis has justified only 40 percent of the operations. Gynecologists' attitudes seem to be: "When in doubt, take out everything and then we will see what the trouble was" (Bosquet, 1974). Surgeons do not have the same attitude about men's reproductive organs or any other part of a man's body. At middle age, women's obsolescence as sex objects is dramatically sealed by an unwarranted hysterectomy reminiscent of primitive tribal rituals.

The treatment of women as objects has been clearly underscored in traditional societies in which brides are bought and sold. When a husband pays a father in order to be granted possession of his wife (*mohr*), as is true in Islamic countries, the transaction is exactly the same as that used in buying a rug, a vase, or a horse. The higher the status of the father, the more beautiful the girl, the better her housekeeping skills, the greater the price the husband is willing to pay. However, the more a man pays for his wife the more he tends to view her as an expensive object rather than as a human being. The investment of a considerable sum of money leads him to expect much "use" out of her in terms of housekeeping services, sex, children, and undivided attention.

In countries in which a dowry was or is paid by the father to the future husband, the rationale was again clear. A wife was an expensive object to maintain and the father had to subsidize the husband to convince him to undertake the maintenance responsibility. The usual negotiations and the quarrels that accompanied these negotiations made women objects to be transferred from one owner to the other. Each side tried to maximize the bargaining position by highlighting crucial advantages or shortcomings having to do with age, beauty, virginity, good reputation, housekeeping skills, health, etc. Women thus measured their own worth by the amount of dowry given to them. A considerable dowry gave a woman standing with her husband and in-laws and a source of power. A very small or no dowry made a woman feel rejected and devalued by her parents, and her feelings were intensified by the demeaning way she was treated by her in-laws. Throughout life she was reminded that she was not important as a person.

Finally, as we have seen, in many traditional societies, the "object" status of women has been clearly underscored by the fact that inappropriate sexual behavior reflected upon the "honor" of her close male relatives, who could kill her in order to "wash away" the dishonor with blood. She was not even allowed to react to her own dishonor.* Male relatives could again determine her fate and dispose of her life. She was like an "object" that proves to be unworthy to be owned, and that has to be disposed of in

---

*Even in these cases, when "dishonored" by her own inappropriate sexual behavior, it was a man's sexual behavior that dishonored her and she was the passive recipient.

order not to embarrass and dishonor the owners! Such "honor crimes" are still taking place in rural Greece (Safilios-Rothschild, 1972), Sicily, and all the Arab countries. Moreover, existing traditional norms in these countries still justify men's behavior and lead to minimum sentences when they chastise women. Thus, in many societies women are still "objects" who are not only used, but who may also be abused, mutilated, or destroyed.

Women's Evaluation of Themselves

When women are consistently used as objects by those around them, it is natural that their self-concept is influenced. The image of women as objects to be displayed, observed, and evaluated has been continuously reinforced by the commercial use of attractive women with sexy looks to sell all kinds of products (Israel and Eliasson, 1971).* Women in ads as well as those displayed in "girlie" magazines project an ideal, perfectly proportioned beauty that only a very small percentage of women can match in real life. Consequently many women do not like their bodies because they do not fit the popular image. They become motivated to spend enormous time, energy, and money trying to beautify themselves, to correct or cover physical shortcomings — in short, to please men. A large and complex business superstructure has been developed around this abnormal preoccupation with perfection and youth. But the emphasis has been more on how to *look* sexy and attractive than on how to *be* sexy (Millum, 1975). Women have learned from all these messages that the facade is what counts and from adolescence on they keep experimenting till they find the most flattering one (Millum, 1975). They add false eyelashes, padded bras, and as much makeup as their skin will tolerate. Ideal beauty correctives have been those that are

---

*Men's bodies have not been used in the same commercial sense. When for the first time an attractive nude young man was used in a magazine ad for men's underwear, men were shocked and resentful (Valabrèque, 1968).

permanent, such as false eyelashes that you can wear to bed so you can wake up looking beautiful. In this way you never have to face your ugly you (Gubbay, 1973). And in their desperate effort to look beautiful, women often become estranged from themselves. Their facade becomes their "real" self; their identity suffers because they learn to define themselves only in terms of their looks. They come to accept a self-image which is empty and shallow and can last only as long as youth, massage, face lifting, and cosmetics can keep it going.

Lipman-Blumen (1976) argues that "women have been forced to fashion themselves as sex objects to attract men and distract them away from other men." Women, forced to attract men since only through them could they get a "piece of the pie," have had to become sex objects (rather than intelligent, brilliant conversationalists) because sexuality is the only "hot" and desirable commodity over which women have exclusive rights. It is common sense, therefore, for them to enhance as much as possible their sexual selves and to "sell" an attractive image of a sex object. Men can always find in other men all the interesting conversations, the friendships, the lively companions, and the fun they need. This is especially true in developing societies where men have often lived most of their lives in the separate world of men and where women have had to compete with male friends for men's attention.

Many women have come to believe that the only way to "catch" a man is by becoming a desirable sex object. This is poignantly illustrated by the strippers and waitresses studied by Gubbay (1976). They feel that "if you are a woman, you might as well show what you've got," and they believe in the potency of the formula: "get a new hairdo, buy a new dress, go on a diet: some day you'll meet Prince Charming who will marry and take care of you for the rest of your life." And they go on displaying different attractive selves, different masks for sale.

Interestingly enough, men have for centuries dictated the types of fashions that women had to follow, subjecting women to most absurd as well as uncomfortable and impractical styles.

Women have obeyed faithfully, spending money and making great sacrifices in order to follow the prevailing laws of attractiveness. One year they let their hair grow long and the next they cut it short. One year their dresses must be full and long and the next year tight and slinky. They must look romantic, mysterious, and exciting today and tomorrow adolescent, innocent, and impish. And women have followed and twisted their looks and their personalities to meet the changing requirements of male-dominated fashion and beauty credos.

The tortures and even deformations to which women have subjected themselves in order to meet men's standards of beauty are not just contemporary and Western phenomena. Chinese women, especially those of well-to-do families, were tortured for centuries by having their feet bound for years until they became smaller and anatomically distorted so that these women could no longer walk normally. They suffered excruciating pain in childhood by having their feet bound, and their anatomical disfiguration became a symbol of femininity, submission, beauty, and distinction as well as a source of erotic pleasure to the male (Chan, 1970). In more recent times, special fattening jellies were sold with great success in Egypt, to guarantee a woman's transformation to a desirable and plump beauty. In Western societies, particularly the U.S., it is not necessary to elaborate on the deprivation and damage to women's health resulting from endless struggles to become slim and hence youthful and desirable. They undergo painful nose operations; they have silicone injections to achieve larger- and firmer-than-life breasts; they even undergo special operations to have fat removed from their body. Where can one find men who have similarly mutilated and endangered their bodies in order to please women?

In the case of men, fashions have tended to change less drastically so that they have had a chance to adjust and to effectively incorporate changes in their self-image (Valabrèque, 1968). This has lessened the possibility of alienation from their own image; they have been able to maintain the feeling (or the illusion) that *they* determined the way they look rather than being puppets run by remote control. This feeling of independence and of self-confidence has been enhanced in men by the fact that there have been no standards of beauty that changed from year to year. A man's attractiveness is seldom determined or significantly dependent upon his looks.* Other characteristics such as occupation, degree of financial and occupational success, reputation and prestige, and personality are important determinants of a man's attractiveness. The expectation of men to succeed in achieving prestige and money has sometimes put enough stress upon men to dehumanize them in some ways. But it did not necessarily transform them into objects. Farrell (1975) claims, however, that, at least within the American context in which success has been glorified, men have been so much judged and evaluated by women on the basis of the extent of their occupational success (that is, money, prestige, and power) that many have become "success objects." This may be true in the American case in which the pursuit of success may have alienated men. It is less true for other societies less haunted by success, partly because success is extremely difficult to achieve and partly because men are not socialized to expect it as a prerequisite for happiness and fulfillment.

Recently, partially because of the influence of the "hippie" countercultures, men have started paying more attention to their appearance; their fashions have become more decorative, colorful, and diverse. Men more often now buy and use colognes (the sales have doubled); they are more concerned about staying trim; and are increasingly becoming the target of ads that try to convince them to use a variety of products in order to appear more "masculine" or in order to look more attractive (Valabrèque, 1968; Sullerot, 1970). Even so, men's fashions still do not change drastically from one extreme to another, and the emerging trends tend to free men from earlier masculine restraints concerning their appearance rather than to alienate them from themselves.

*Many women tend to mistrust and not become attracted to very good-looking men; they may suspect them of being homosexuals or "womanizers."

Women's great preoccupation with their appearance and the fashions that can enhance their attractiveness is but a symptom of a larger "feminine" syndrome of other-directedness and the need to be liked. "Feminine" socialization conditions women to please other people and depend upon this approval. From a very young age, men are approved and liked when they achieve, but women can be liked, regardless of achievement, if they are willing to conform to what others want them to do. In this way, their socialization has prepared them to be content with their subordinate position in the society. But at the same time, it has also tended to alienate them from themselves as human beings. Many women have never developed strong preferences, wishes, likes, and dislikes but instead have gone along with whatever others wanted in order to please and accommodate them. Many have done things just to please others (although they often hated doing it) for so long that they finally lost sight of what they wanted or who they were. Displeasing the man they loved could throw such women into a state of depression and arouse considerable anxiety and fear of rejection. It seems that this need to please others and particularly to please the men they love is a very deep-seated element in women's socialization; it has proved difficult to overcome even after awareness has been raised through the women's movement ideology. Usually, the present generations of adult "liberated" women can learn that they do not have to please their colleagues and co-workers and all their friends and relatives all the time, although even this learning process is painful. But once they love a man, they have tremendous difficulty in overcoming their socialized tendency to do anything to please him and win his approval, a tendency that often backfires.

The present gradual rebellion of women against their male-oriented socialization seems to be threatening to many who fear the social and psychological consequences. The *Total Woman* book and workshops represent the counter-current to the liberation movement, encouraging women to go back to being desirable and pleasant sex objects and "servants" if they want to keep their man (Bernard, 1971).

The crucial question that needs to be raised is: Can women

who are viewed by men and view themselves as "sex objects" really love and be loved? It is true that people can become very fond of things and that these things can occupy a very central place in their lives. But when one loves an object, one does not expect love in return. It is possible that men have loved women in the same way, without the expectation of any substantial reciprocation. This may explain why some men have felt threatened, uncomfortable, and overwhelmed when the women they loved fully returned their love. A recent analysis of the images of woman in the mass media in England showed that the relationship between the male and female portrayed in ads is often one-sided: "It is a relationship in which the man is giving his attention to the woman while she is interested elsewhere, and that elsewhere is often herself" (Millum, 1975). One can be infatuated with an object, since infatuation does not need reciprocity. But one cannot love an object in a mature way. Mature love is based on human interaction and a mutual desire and effort to understand and love.

In the case of women, even more serious questions can be raised about their ability to express and enjoy their sexuality and to experience mature, fulfilling relationships. While some could argue that in some cases sex may be quite as good in a master-slave relationship as in any other, the fact remains that the powerless position of women may sometimes transform sexuality into another form of masculine oppression. Furthermore, it is clear that freedom is necessary if a person is to determine his/her life and to commit him/herself to a love relationship with another human being. The type of ownership and disregard for human feelings and emotions that has characterized male-female relationships for centuries have not been conducive to the development of love. As we shall see in the next chapter, women treated as slaves and sex objects often objectified men in return, seeing them as a type of sexual machine that could assure money, status, and protection.

Three

MEN AS OBJECTS
The Vengeance of the Victim

We have seen in the last chapter that women traditionally have been viewed as objects. However, in examining the extent to which human beings can "objectify" each other, it is important to look at the means by which women try to "get back at" men for the way they have been treated. This "vengeance" of the traditional "victim," often unconsciously implemented, takes different forms. In this chapter we will discuss two of the most common: the diminution of men to objects to be manipulated sexually, and the treatment of men as children.

Men as Sex Objects

In general, it can be argued that from the moment men treat women as objects, they also become dehumanized and leave themselves open to reciprocal treatment. Women also objectify men by reducing them to money-making machines, appreciation and love of them increasing with the amount of money they earn (and spend on women).

This type of objectification leads to a special dehumanization of men, whose attractiveness has little to do with physical appearance or personality but is mainly based on their earning ability, their prestige and power. Of course, some personality characteristics are involved in men's capacity to earn money and become successful — such as competitiveness, intelligence and astuteness, perseverance and hard work — but they are hardly the characteristics which are crucial to or facilitate love relationships. Men in traditional societies as well as in the contemporary U.S. often internalize this type of objectification and do not dare aspire to a "desirable" woman unless they have the type of job and level of income considered satisfactory in their social class. Thus, men often internalize this dehumanizing definition of attractiveness and "sexiness" imposed upon them by women. It is only recently that American men have started realizing this and rebelling against the fact that some women are attracted to them or "love" them because they are successful rather than because of the type of person they are (Goldberg, 1976).

Men's objectification in terms of money, status, and power accomplishments has been more particularly a middle- and upper-middle-class phenomenon. Low-income men have most often escaped this particular type of objectification, since they have usually had little access to these societal "goodies," but they too, perhaps even more acutely, have been viewed and treated as "sex machines." Thus, the sexual, child-like objectification of men cuts across all classes, and we shall examine it in more detail.

THE ART OF SEXUAL TEASING

In societies in which sex-role stereotypes have predominated and the sexual double standard has been strictly enforced (e.g., in Latin American, Mediterranean and Middle Eastern societies), sexual "teasing" has been prevalent.* This is an art in which females sexually entice and tempt men while withholding sexual satisfaction (Fabian, 1973). Sexual teasing can be seen as an adaptation by women to their social and their sexual oppression. In such traditional societies, women are prohibited from sex before marriage, as we have seen. But while they must withhold sex, they want to keep men sexually interested in them. They must find ways to attract men, and to be so desirable that men will be willing to give up their freedom in order to possess women sexually. In a sense, sexual "teasing" has allowed women to "have their cake and eat it, too."

Women have always been carefully groomed from a tender age in the intricate art of sexual teasing. They have been taught how to make themselves attractive, desirable, and provocative; how to dress, stand, speak, and behave in a tempting way. Fashion, cosmetics, perfumes, and a whole world of manufacturers and consultants have developed in order to help women look sexy and alluring according to men's definitions at any particular time. Women have spent enormous amounts of time and energy in the pursuit of this goal. But in doing so, they removed themselves further from a realistic and healthy self-concept and often became alienated and estranged from themselves.

Women have likewise been carefully trained to "turn off" and become sexually inaccessible when men, encouraged by the "come-on," desire them and want to make love to them. This aspect of their socialization has been much more difficult and once in a while, because it presupposes considerable control and discipline over sexual impulses and needs, it has failed. In order for women to be able effectively to withhold sex from men to whom they are attracted, they must be taught not to desire a man sexually but only to dream of him in a romantic sense. In this way, attraction is expressed in terms of love and not in terms of sexual desire.

---

*The same is true for social groups that strictly adhere to the double sexual standard—such as the Italian-American, the Greek-American (at least in the first and second generation), or the rural and low-income populations in many societies.

Teasing can be much more effective in traditional societies in which men, especially unmarried young men, have little opportunity or possibility to interact socially with women. This increases their view of women as sex objects and whets their appetite. They are driven by the unavailability of sex to want to follow, flirt with, touch all women. With this attitude men do not learn to relate to women as human beings and they do not understand them; the only way to relate to them is sexually. Within this context, women's teasing goes a long way. Usually, the more the associations with women, the less successful the effects of teasing. Playboy bunnies and strippers, who are professional "teasers," indicate, however, that considerable numbers of men are still hungry enough to stare night after night at women's bodies (Gubbay, 1976).

As women have learned how to sexually "tease" men, they have often expressed considerable pleasure in being able to attract and tempt them and then rebuff them or keep them at a distance. This has given many women a rare, if not unique, sense of power over men. In such cases men are rendered more or less powerless and dependent according to the intensity of their desire. Since women could better control the situation when they were not themselves involved, they sometimes sexually teased men to whom they were not at all attracted in order to obtain special privileges or just to test their power or to amuse themselves. Thus, sexual teasing can be a powerful and dangerous weapon in the hands of some women. And many women have enjoyed the game so much that they have deliberately chosen to stay unmarried; others marry and continue the game after marriage. In some social strata, teasing goes on at cocktail parties, dinners, and other social occasions. Beautifully dressed and adorned women tease others' husbands and escorts. And some men seem to enjoy seeing their wife desired but unattainable to other men; this reassures them that they possess a valuable sex object!

The exercise of sexual teasing has had some definite effects upon women's (and possible also men's) sexuality as well as upon their self-concept and their ability to love. Women have been taught how to look but not how *to be* sexually attractive or how to adequately function sexually. Often their superficial cover of sexual attractiveness becomes a substitute for real sexuality. Women, well-trained in playing the challenging and sometimes cruel sexual game, are not equally well-equipped to behave sexually when the game stops and it is time for actual consummation. Skilled in withholding sex, women have not been socialized to be equally skilled in engaging in it or enjoying it. In fact they have been often almost totally unprepared for real sexuality. Furthermore, sexual teasing prepares women well to manipulate sex as a commodity in marriage, as we shall discuss in the next section. Many women, after concentrating long on the trappings of sex and withholding its actual practice, become alienated from their own sexuality and find that they are unable to "let themselves go" and enjoy sex for its own sake.

Teasing has made many women concentrate almost totally on "winning" men's approval and love (and lust). Under these conditions, it sometimes becomes immaterial whether they love or feel attracted to a man; the important thing is to get the man to "fall" for them. On the way they may lose themselves by never appearing as they *are* but as they are most appealing to men (Gubbay, 1976; Greer, 1972) — and in the bargain, lose the ability to love.

One can question how women's sexual teasing has affected men's sexuality and, more specifically, whether or not in some cases it has tended to reduce them also to sex objects. Sexual teasing has developed because of the assumption that males are necessarily sexually aroused by *any* woman who is attractive, desirable, and available; all men, in this view, are interested primarily in sexual conquest. Other types of social, moral, humanistic, and affective considerations play a secondary role. This type of assumption sells a man short as a human being; it is debasing and humiliating and actually reduces men to the status of sex objects. Furthermore, the arousal of men by sexual teasing and the subsequent denial of the opportunity to realize their sexual desires has placed many men in a position in which they could be conditioned, manipulated for someone else's ends. It can be further argued that sexual teasing has rendered some men powerless* by restricting their interaction with women within the "feminine" confines of sexuality—affection and desire expressed by exciting touching and kissing without ever entering the more "masculine" domain of sexual consummation.

Because men often resent the frustration, humiliation, and powerlessness experienced through sexual teasing by women, they have occasionally reacted vindictively and/or violently. Traditionally, men have been socialized to feel powerful and dominant over a woman only when they have dominated her sexually. Retaliation for men who have been used by women has been in the form of calling on their social power over the woman and clearly reducing her through punishment to her "properly" subordinate position. One way of gaining revenge has been ruining her reputation—for instance, spreading the rumor that a woman who has in fact only "teased" a man has actually had sexual relations with him. Such an accusation often represented a powerful punishment in traditional societies in which the honor and thus the marketability of women could be destroyed by a bad reputation. More aggressive men have paid women back by using force to have sexual relations. Actually, we must not forget that many of the rape laws even now in these United States reflect exactly this type of situation. In a sense, current rape laws can be seen as representing men's efforts to protect themselves legally for the kind of forceful behavior to which they often succumb when they have been extremely frustrated by the sexual teasing of women.

While the extreme form of sexual teasing is found in its purity mainly in traditional societies, the practice has certainly not been discontinued. It has only changed form. Many women, though they are still socialized to appear sexy, desirable, and at-

*Some objections can be raised as to whether men have ever been reduced to powerless sex objects through women's sexual teasing. Some say that men can sexually control and dominate women and, therefore, their powerlessness is at best only partial. Even so, a woman who uses a man sexually to gain her own ends may annihilate a man's power potential over her by refusing him sexual access.

tractive, and to play endless, complicated "indifference" games with men, no longer feel obligated to withhold sex. But still, the "granting" of sex has to be well-timed, and only after the man has shown a serious interest or has made certain serious emotional commitments (Walshok, 1973). Most women still play the "temptress" role and try being sexy and enticing with "plastic" feelings rather than being warm, giving, and loving women. They still concentrate their energies on developing a panoply of sexual wiles at the expense of building a mature and honest knowledge of themselves and other people.

SEX AS A COMMODITY

As we have seen, when women are treated as sex objects in most, if not all, man-woman relationships, the temptation is considerable for them to use sex in order to manipulate men to get what they want. This temptation is even greater when women control few other valuable resources. In fact, whenever women have little direct access to money, prestige, and power, they are not only tempted but are even forced to use sex as their only weapon, their only resource (Coleman, 1966; Safilios-Rothschild, 1976). Only by using sexuality as a tool can they diminish the social distance between themselves and men and gain access to money and prestige and occasionally also to power. The ability, however, to effectively give or withhold sex in order to get something does not work unless the man involved is really quite anxious to have sexual relations. Obviously, the less desirable a man finds a woman, the less he suffers from her withholding sex, and the less the woman can use sex instrumentally. This explains why in most societies and throughout most of history many women have been careful to marry a man whose love and desire was stronger than their own.* In this way sex as a resource took

*Even when women had little decision-making power as to whom they would marry, parents usually chose a man who cared very much about their daughter because such a choice often offered them financial advantages (when, for example, the fiancé demanded little or no dowry), but possibly also because they felt that their daughter would be better off in such a marriage.

on much greater value, since it was very much desired by the man. In this respect any woman who married a man she loved as much or more than he loved her had a great handicap in that she could not effectively use sex. Studies both in the United States and in Greece have shown clearly that the withdrawal or granting of sex at a critical point has been used by wives quite consciously and effectively in order to influence husbands (Safilios-Rothschild, 1976).

However, withholding sex can be a tricky business in traditional societies in which women have a very low social position and in marriages in which there is no love. In this situation, women are often afraid to withhold sex because the man can and sometimes does find another sexual partner. In these cases, sex is not a valuable resource controlled by the wife. Prostitutes and "bad" women have been easily accessible to these men who have a low opinion of women in general and/or do not allow themselves to become used by their wives. Otherwise, women can be interchangeable sex objects, as long as they are attractive and desirable. Love must be at least to some degree integrated with sexuality in the minds of men before sex with a particular woman can be considered desirable.

The use of sex by women to get what they want from men (money, status, prestige, or power) represents the ultimate dehumanization of sexual relations. It is clearly impossible for sex to be mature and fulfilling under such conditions. It must be pointed out, however, that men, in this instance, are much more the victims than women since it is men's sexual needs and desires that are being manipulated and utilized. We must also realize that the reason for this type of humiliation and objectification of both men and sexual relations is that women have been almost totally alienated by the fact that they have not had the right to demand things they want. They have not been able to exert power; nor have they had direct access to many resources; they simply have not been *entitled* to be forceful or dominant. It is only because women have been so totally deprived of many of the desirable goods in society and of any direct power that some have resorted to manipulation and trickery to get a share of what is rightfully due them, or just in order to survive.

Here again it is important to note that in order for women to be successful in manipulating sex as a resource, they must either not really care very much about sex in itself or they must be able to separate sex from love and enjoy sex without becoming emotionally and affectively vulnerable. In the first case, sex must cease being for them an inherently desirable relationship. This devaluation of sex may be easy for women socialized to believe that their sexual drives are very low, if they exist at all, and that sex is not important for women or even that it is shameful for women to have strong sexual drives. Historically, women have been persuaded that they are able to live with little and only occasional sex. Therefore, they have had to train themselves not to desire men sexually—otherwise their whole ability to withhold sex and to manipulate men would be seriously jeopardized. Under such conditions, it is really very difficult to expect that sexual relations could be satisfactory for either men or women. Sex has been used as a commodity, and consequently women have directly victimized men as well as themselves.

In the second case, women have effectively used sex as an influence technique by separating sexual satisfaction and love feelings. Many know how to give a lot of sexual pleasure to a man—in fact, enjoy the act tremendously themselves. As long as they can remain sentimentally detached or can control their feelings and emotions, they can use sex to manipulate men. But this separation, this dehumanization of the sexual relationship, is only possible when sex is not embedded in love but is carefully kept (at least by women) within the confines of desire and physical pleasure. In fact, some women have been known to prefer marrying the man who loves them very much (and more than they love him) to the man they love, since in the latter case their emotions would interfere with their ability to manipulate him sexually (Safilios-Rothschild, 1975). This is, ironically enough, playing the sex game according to masculine rules, avoiding the "feminine" world of feelings and emotions within which men have been socialized to feel uncomfortable. Nonetheless, in this game men are mere sex *objects,* women are calculating operators, and both are losers.

In traditional societies in which women have not been socialized to enjoy sex or to become skilled in lovemaking, only two categories of women have been free to enjoy the sex act and to be skilled in lovemaking: "bad" women who, as we shall see in Chapter 4, were therefore viewed as *femmes fatales* because of the sexual power and psychological independence they possessed; and wealthy women who, in most traditional and present-day developing nations, have typically been exempt from social, psychological, and sexual restrictions imposed on all other women (Safilios-Rothschild, 1974). It is not accidental that the movie portrayals of "bad" women today in Greece include mainly wealthy women whose economic and social independence has brought them considerable psychological and sexual freedom and independence (Safilios-Rothschild, 1972).

Men as Children

Women have often reduced men to objects by treating them as children rather than as adults. Whether conscious or unconscious, this has been a significant vengeance on the part of the victim because it robs men of their seriousness and importance. But it must be noted from the beginning that women have seldom done this *openly.* Rather, they have pretended to agree that men really were the powerful figures who alone shouldered all the responsibilities, solved the difficult problems, and made all the important decisions. But secretly (or with other women) they have seen men as big children who had to be humored, cajoled, caressed, reprimanded, cared for, even "broken in" to marriage, but never taken totally seriously. Such women may not pay attention to or believe what men promise, plan, or dream. They believe that men are childlike in their outlook on life and they, therefore, dismiss men's often grandiose ideas, plans, and promises. Women have also realized that sometimes men, despite their appearance of being competent, efficient, rational and sharp, are not able to predict clearly and accurately the complications and difficulties involved in their projects and plans and tend to be overwhelmed by the eventual social and psychological complications that develop. Because women have such a "childlike" mental picture of men, their typical behavior is to "spoil" men, cater to them; love and pamper them; help them while at the same time make them feel important and give them all the credit; and protect them from interpersonal problems and complications as well as failures and unpleasant situations. Thus some women take on the role of the mother. When the child-husband comes home from work this kind of woman may put on a mask of false cheerfulness and happiness so that the man (boy) will be sheltered from pain and difficulty—and reality. Of course, husbands have to face the difficulties and complications of work, as children must also do at school. And men's socialization has prepared them to cope with many responsibilities and difficulties. But unfortunately, many men have not been adequately prepared to deal with emotions, fears, weaknesses. They have not even been allowed in many cases to admit them. A wife who regards men as grown-up children continues this overprotection and insulation from reality. Thus many men never are allowed to fully develop psychologically and emotionally as adults. They are handicapped emotionally and grow to feel comfortable only with women who protect them as their mothers did. They need women who do not challenge them and do not force them to face themselves.

The more traditional model has been for wives to continue the idealization process started by mothers. Especially in traditional societies, mothers have often brought up their sons to believe that they are unique, perfect, "God's gift to humanity." It is understandable that such men seek out women who reinforce this image by offering them the same unconditional admiration and idealization. Surprisingly, this phenomenon is sometimes found even among "modern," sophisticated people living in dual-career marriages: the same one-way, psychological dependence of the husband; the same mothering and overprotection by the wife.

Many such men become attracted to and fall in love with women who treat them as adults rather than as children—that is, women who expect some reciprocity in terms of psychological dependence. Such women may excite them, but the growing-up process usually is too painful; they find it too difficult to face themselves, their shortcomings, and the realities of life. Finding the relationship too demanding and taxing, they retreat to a relationship in which they can feel comfortable by being treated as unique and perfect children.

Women have also reduced men to childlike objects by running everything smoothly and efficiently—in their own way. Men, often tired from work and too lazy to object or make changes, have submitted to the organization and structure imposed by the wife at home and even more generally permeating their lives. This has, for some men, proved an easier course than inventing and implementing other plans. In time, many men are finally defeated in any small rebellions against the authority of their wives. The same reasons most often prevent them from leaving for another woman. Even love and desire often lose to comfort and the security of a well-organized life with a woman who is willing to shoulder responsibility for the difficulties of life, even if it means accepting her authority and conforming to her rules and regulations. We are all too familiar with the images capitalized upon by cartoons of an important executive or a respected professor who, upon crossing the threshhold of his home, reverts to childhood and feels naughty whenever he does what he wants rather than what his wife expects him to do.

Women have commonly found it easier to "handle" men after they have usurped or thwarted their adult status. By reducing them to children, they do not have to deal with the complicated web of feelings, emotions, needs, reactions, and desires of an adult. They only have to satisfy elementary emotional, psychological, sexual, and physical needs. And surprisingly, this oversimplified model of manhood has "worked" in many cases.

The important question is: Why has it worked? Is it because these men never had the chance to grow up, having always been sheltered? Or is it because it relaxed them and offered them a much-needed balance with the usual all-powerful and self-reliant masculine image they had to present to the world? Or is it further because this child-like reliance on women in some areas allowed them to concentrate their efforts on the occupational, political, religious, and military arenas on which their worth is judged? Probably a combination of these has been operating, but not necessarily at the conscious level. Whatever the mechanisms and dynamics by which some men have come to be viewed and treated as children by women, this process has represented a contradiction to their traditional role. In being treated as children, in allowing women to minimize their importance and manipulate them in order to satisfy their own needs, these men have surrendered not only their position of dominance and power, they have allowed themselves to be diminished as human beings. They have become less, having submitted to the machinations of women who themselves, in so behaving, also make themselves less.

What about masculinity? Where does it fit in the discussion of men as objects? Stereotypic "masculine" men are not adults, they are tough children who were never helped and allowed to grow. Hence, masculinity cannot necessarily be equated with adulthood. Today, when women complain that they cannot find "real" men, they do not mean tough, masculine men; they mean *adult* men. Adult men are few. By "adult" they mean men who know who they are, who are aware and can face their emotions, their vulnerabilities, their shortcomings, and the complications of everyday life. Moreover, they mean men who are ready to accept reciprocal relationships in which both partners can freely give and receive love and sexual caring. Mature love demands two individuals who do not use sex to control, dominate, manipulate, or humiliate others. In the next chapter we will look at some of the major obstacles to developing such a love relationship.

Four

OBSTACLES TO
THE DEVELOPMENT OF LOVE

*The Dehumanization
of Love and Sex*

We have seen that the social inequality between men and women, the stereotyped masculinity and femininity and the resulting sexual double standard have tended to dehumanize the relationships between men and women. This dehumanization has created several major obstacles to the development of love: (1) the separation of sexuality from love; (2) the inability of men and women to meet and deal with each other openly and honestly; (3) the incompatibility of traditional definitions of masculinity and femininity with the idea of love as an intimate, rewarding human relationship.

THE SEPARATION OF LOVE AND SEX

Men and women have experienced in different ways the separation of sex from love. We have already discussed how, in traditional societies, women have been socialized to refuse sex before marriage regardless of the intensity of experienced love. A man could prove his genuine love for a woman by marrying her and, supposedly, merging love and sexuality. In reality, often the sexual needs of neither were satisfied within the marriage and the wife learned to repress even more her sexuality, while the husband sought fulfilling sex elsewhere. Since marriage as a proof of love often entailed considerable social and economic sacrifice on the part of men, they sometimes asked women to prove their love by having sex before marriage. If both felt a real love, the result was generally a destructive guilt. In the case of a man merely seeking sexual gratification, the woman who was naive enough to comply was devalued, viewed as a "fallen," "bad" woman and usually abandoned by the man, who no longer esteemed or loved her (Parca, 1968). "Good" women were supposed to withstand sexual temptations before marriage and to successfully separate love from sexuality.* "Good" women were socialized to suppress their sexual needs — sex was supposed to be dirty and degrading unless "cleansed" by love within marriage. So when such women felt sexual desires, they never dared admit them for the fear that they might then be viewed as "bad." Any who attempted to integrate love and sexuality before marriage were more than likely to be deprived of both marriage and love. Moreover, any sexual contacts they had were likely to be without love. The "bad" women who chose to enjoy sex without accepting the socially imposed standards were occasionally both exciting and threatening

*Occasionally "good" girls who had sex before marriage managed not to lose their good reputation by making it seem as though their behavior was not their fault, blaming it on external factors beyond their control, such as magic, spells, or sleep as a symbolic state of helplessness. The folklore of traditional cultures refers to such cases (Safilios-Rothschild, 1965).

to traditional men, who have usually been quite ambivalent toward "bad" women.

Interestingly enough, while "good" women had to abstain from sex before marriage even when they were in love, once married, they were expected to *accept* sex, whether it was accompanied by feelings of love or not. As Lipman-Blumen (1975) points out, marriage has been expected to magically transform sex from sin to an expression of love! It was a wife's duty to have sexual relations (but not to enjoy sex) with her husband, even when the separation of sex from love was so extreme that the wife was totally indifferent or even felt disgust. In this way, because many traditional marriages were not love marriages, through a different set of mechanisms traditional women ended up separating love from sex before *and* after marriage and becoming alienated from both.

Paralleling "good" women's socialization to withhold sex before marriage has been men's conditioning to the idea that women always have to resist having sexual relations. Women's resistance is seen as necessary and the result of this is a struggle between the woman's asexual virtue and the man's overt sexual needs. Some men adapt to this by actually enjoying the fact that women give them a hard time. Some men with masculinity hangups report that they find it exciting and stimulating to have sexual relations with a woman who resists them and even fights them off. When a traditional man tries to initiate sexual relations with a woman, he may not accept the validity of her refusal. Even though he knows that this is a socially appropriate response because of his "masculinity" image, he may be convinced that she really wants to have sex with him but must at first refuse him in order to prove that she is moral. Therefore, in some cases the forcing of sexual relations upon nonconsenting women represents only a slight extension of the belief that a woman's refusal is only a socially acceptable or, alternatively, a sexually exciting response and not a valid denial. Rape is only a few steps removed from this rationale. Some men rape their girlfriends or wives exactly within this context and because of these motivations.

Men, unlike women, have commonly been able to have both sex without love and love without sex relatively easily and without social disapproval. In traditional contexts, sex without love has not been unusual; it has often represented the first sexual experience, with prostitutes or "bad" women not eligible to become wives (Parca, 1968). The more traditional the prevailing sex-role stereotypes and segregation of the sexes, the more extreme is the separation of sex and love. A study done in rural Morocco where young, unmarried men have no access whatsoever to love and sexual relationships with "good" women showed that they resort to masturbation, sodomy, homosexuality, prostitutes, and even bestiality for sexual expression (Pascon and Bentahar, 1969). Because these men have had to learn to function sexually entirely under such dehumanizing conditions, they were subsequently viewed as entirely sexual beings aroused by all kinds of sexual stimuli *in the absence of* love, warmth, or affection. In fact, traditional-type men are often thought of as sexual "machines" that can function regardless of the social, psychological, or moral context. Partly through a self-fulfilling prophecy, some traditional men eventually become just that (Parca, 1968).

The often-imposed separation of sex from love before marriage sometimes culminates in the dehumanizing of men's sexual desires to such a degree that all love relationships are affected. If a man entirely segregates sex from love and still manages to function "normally" for a sustained period of time, he may lose the ability to love in a whole and realistic way. Many Southern Italian men, for example, have admitted that when they love and marry a woman, they often then deemphasize the sexual relationship as an expression of love and respect for that woman. It is as if they feel that the full integration of sexuality in this relationship would degrade it. Thus, they continue to satisfy sexual needs mainly through separate relationships with prostitutes or temporary liaisons (Parca, 1968). Traditional Greek men of all ages and classes, on the other hand, who have had to pretend and eloquently profess their love in order to have sexual access to a woman they desired, often become totally inarticulate with the woman they love. The reputation of the Mediterranean and Latin "lover" has probably come from the fact that some traditional men have learned to express their feelings (mostly desire) in such flowery and romantic style that many a Northern woman loses her head while local women learn to disregard and, in fact, to mistrust such facile speeches. Having had to manipulate and lie about their emotions and to simulate love for too long, such men often find themselves at a loss when it comes to expressing themselves to a true love.

LACK OF MUTUAL TRUST

The second important dehumanizing influence on love relationships has been the fact that men and women have not been able to feel free and comfortable with each other. The result is that openness and honesty are difficult or impossible. The socialization process encourages play-acting, creating the expected images rather than establishing honest human relationships. People become objects in the intricate power and sex games that are played. Men have tried to dominate women, and winning means total sexual submission. Women have sought to "win" by presenting themselves as coy, weak, hard-to-get (Farrell, 1975). Once a woman becomes attainable, once she submits sexually, the man often loses interest in her exactly when she is the most vulnerable and psychologically dependent upon him. In this way, "his masculinity is being measured by the degree to which he robs women of both their humanity and their sexuality and robs himself of the ability to be human" (Farrell, 1975). Women who have been treated this way often end up hating men and wanting revenge more than a good relationship. Most traditional women learned their lesson from the mistakes of a few and successfully played their game of sexual teasing regardless of the sexual desires and attraction they felt until they married. Marriage, implying the tying down of a man to a particular woman, marked woman's victory in the love-sex game. This pattern has been more clear-cut within traditional societies and subgroups in which the lack of contact and understanding between men and women often led to considerable hatred and animosity. Men perceived women as petty, sneaky, scheming, untrustworthy, and dangerous (Farrell, 1975). Women saw men as sex-hungry "wolves," irresponsible, insensitive, cruel, domineering, and exploitative. And the war of the sexes rages. How can anyone really love within this context?

In societies in which the sexual double standard is no longer so rigidly enforced and in which the traditional stereotypes do not operate so strongly, it is no longer possible for women to completely and consistently put off sex until marriage. But this does not end the game — it merely changes it. And the game continues to be dehumanizing. Women have to continuously play an elusive role, presenting themselves as much desired, irresistible, in order to excite the competitive spirit in the men they love. Even when they "capture" a man they still have to continue to tease and challenge him to sustain his sexual and affective interest. Women, thus, can never show their real feelings, the extent to which they really love, and the extent to which they may feel need or dependence. Women can never relax, be themselves, let down their defenses and enjoy relationships. They have to be always on guard not to "lose out" in the relationship. They have to be sure to win the "upmanship" game by not showing any emotional weakness or vulnerability and by preserving an aura of mystery, uncertainty and fleetingness, even with partially "liberated" men.

Men too have been equally concerned with making the "right" moves and with using the "appropriate" strategies that would give them power, dominance, independence, and control. In fact many have turned love and sexuality into means for gaining power and control over women. Such men have fought any perceived emotional weakness and humanity to maintain control of the situation. They have tried hard to maintain an appearance of emotional and psychological invulnerability and independence. Men's "power trips" have interfered with their ability to love, give in to their feelings, and savor love. Men's and women's angles and preoccupations have often made love a tiring and strenuous battlefield into which one could step only fully armed with a panoply of "tricks and treats."

In conclusion, it seems that until recently the more traditional the mentalities and the roles in which men and women have been cast, the more they have viewed each other with mistrust, lack of understanding, and often hatred. Their relationships have become polarized, separating sex and love, making it difficult for people to enjoy warm, trusting, loving and totally human relationships. Within the traditional context, whenever love managed to overcome all hurdles and survive in the midst of hangups and power games, it was a miracle indeed. But even now, when the traditional sex-role stereotypes have started to break down, men and women are still preoccupied with creating images rather than with being themselves. It seems to be very hard to overcome the dehumanization of love and sex because we are still more interested in winning than in enjoying.

THE INCOMPATIBILITY
OF LOVE AND MASCULINITY

The question can be seriously raised as to whether it was ever possible for a man who had been socialized according to a masculine stereotype to really love another human being, and especially a woman. Traditionally, men have been afraid of love because they were afraid that love would rob them of their independence, their toughness, as well as their carefree orientation toward life. It can be argued that love has been by definition incompatible with traditional masculinity in terms of the ability to express feelings, weaknesses, dependence, and attachment. It is interesting that an analysis of popular American songs between 1954 and 1968 (Wilkinson, 1976) showed that men in love were portrayed as crying (even more frequently than women); as needing and being dependent on women; as submissive and helpless; and as faithful and committed. Clearly, the image of men in love projected in these songs is contrary to masculine norms and, therefore, very threatening. The men become emotional, weak, vulnerable, suffering, dependent, and unable to dominate the relationship and the woman they love. These songs portray quite eloquently men's deep-seated fears of love, since when they are in love they can no longer maintain the stereotypic masculine facade of self-control and invulnerability. The seeming incompatibility between love and masculinity is clearly underlined. Love, therefore, is to be avoided as much as possible. Probably the only reason for which men ever allowed themselves to fall in love was that they were challenged by love and their masculine pride made them believe that they could get involved but still remain masters of the situation. *Love's because he's in* (command)

In traditional Muslim societies, love has been seen as downgrading to men, exactly because it was viewed as robbing them of their masculinity (Mernissi, 1973). Furthermore, love was incompatible with the traditional masculine image because it distracted men from their "serious" duties and preoccupations related to work, success, war, and ideologies.* Love represented a competing commitment that pleased women but that absorbed men's energy, thoughts, and feelings. In fact, men's dominating concerns were thought of as helping them tone down their intense emotional involvements by forcing them to function and to control their emotions.

Finally, some behavioral scientists claim that it has been impossible for men to love women as long as masculinity implied a clear-cut superiority over women. This has been especially true in cultures in which the wives were sold to or bought by husbands as an object. As we shall discuss later in this chapter, there are serious doubts as to whether love can exist at all between social unequals.

One of the important measures of masculinity has been a man's ability to "possess" a number of women. Because this

*In Muslim societies, love was viewed as seriously interfering with men's allegiance to Allah, an important masculine duty (Mernissi, 1975).

"possession" was exclusively sexual, it excluded the possibility of love. And the *number* of sexual conquests counted rather than the nature of the relationship. Also important was the "market value" of the sexually conquered objects in terms of age, attractiveness, and virginity (Israel and Eliasson, 1971).

Because the masculine image has always required aggressiveness and the enjoyment of sex, the woman was naturally seen as a passive object and a possession. Thus, a woman who was sexually responsive, or showed any tendency to enjoy or initiate sex, represented a threat to the status quo. Furthermore, the more sexual pleasure that was derived from a particular relationship, the more men were apt to feel vulnerable out of the fear that they might become dependent on this relationship and therefore no longer be able to control and dominate it. This intense fear seriously interfered with men's ability to let themselves love and enjoy loving and being loved.

Men's fear of women's sexual responsiveness is best illustrated in the traditional stigmatization of women as "bad" when their sexual and affective behavior indicated full participation and enjoyment. Movies, books, and songs portray "bad" women as *femmes fatales,* appealing but dangerous and often destructive. A favorite fiction is of the siren who lures the poor man into falling hopelessly in love, drains him of his willpower so that he neglects obligations and responsibilities, and then leaves him a "shadow of his former self." The message is clear — unless men can control their feelings and overpower wicked temptation, their doom is inescapable (Safilios-Rothschild, 1968).

Even when masculine men have managed to love and not run away scared of their own feelings, what has been the meaning of love to them? Masculine sex-role stereotypes often made it difficult even to recognize and express (or admit) their emotions. Many men still find it impossible to say "I love you" even when they feel this emotion (Balswick and Peek, 1970; Balswick and Collier, 1974). The John Wayne type is a celebrated illustration of this masculine difficulty. Love was to be expressed only in terms of the man's desire to marry, protect, and financially support the loved woman (as well as to control and dominate her). Such were the tangible "manly" indications of love. In this masculine love there was seldom the desire to understand or to please the woman (Mernissi, 1975) and the woman's reciprocation of love was not a necessary condition. Love was there to serve the man's needs and to be played according to his rules—rules that sometimes were quite bizarre and one-sided. For example, a man could love a woman but be unfaithful, rude, even violent. A woman had to be faithful, sweet, obedient, and supportive in order to show her love. There were so many exploitative and oppressive elements in this type of love, defined in terms of traditional masculinity, that it could hardly be called an "intimate, rewarding human relationship."

THE INCOMPATIBILITY
OF LOVE AND FEMININITY

But lest we seem to have pounced too hard on the traditional definition of masculinity as a major barrier to the accomplishing of a mature love relationship, we must look at the other side of the coin—the age-old feminine ideal. For hundreds of years men have claimed that they could only love a "feminine" woman. While the definition of "femininity" was often ambiguous, it usually referred to a syndrome of characteristics that included emotionality, passivity, irrationality, dependency, nonaggressiveness, and weakness. In fact, some of the characteristics included in the package of feminine role stereotypes could be conducive to the development and maintenance of a close, loving relationship. Such characteristics include the ability to express emotions, feelings, and weaknesses and to love without being concerned about dominance. Some "feminine" women, however, have occasionally, in their failure to develop an identity of their own, become quite dependent upon the men they loved. And in some cases this overdependence led to possessiveness that crushed the relationship.

In order to "land a man" some women behaved in a way that often led to their emotional and sexual alienation. As we have already seen, women had to "tease" men sexually to create an elusive and desirable image. They feigned indifference, and learned to grant conditional interest and love. These techniques and strategies required skills such as the coyness, craftiness, and guile that have been associated with femininity. Learning well how to utilize such tricks, many women "won" their men at the cost of their own emotional and sexual alienation.

The stereotypic femininity has been incompatible with mature love because it has been used to please men so that they can be made to act according to women's wishes. In this sense, femininity was instrumental. Women used it effectively in order to attract the "right" man; to manipulate men (as objects); to succeed in their goals; and to win some power back from men. In this sense, femininity has been used in the same way as sex but has often had little to do with love; all too often it has been used to incite love in men but not in themselves. Some women make themselves particularly attractive, sweet, and pleasing so that men will fall in love with them, but this does not necessarily mean that they will also fall in love.

Femininity has also implied a slightly enigmatic behavior. A woman who can surround herself with an aura of mystery has typically been considered feminine and attractive. This aspect of femininity is important in brief and exciting love-adventures, but it can hardly be conducive to long-term affectionate and mature love relationships. Finally, femininity has been basically associated with women's status as sex objects. Seldom has a woman ever been considered feminine if she was old, badly dressed, or physically unattractive. Actually, this close association of femininity with the sex-object characteristics of women may constitute the most crucial incompatibility between femininity and love. One can, of course, "love" an art object, a beautiful house, an elegant car, and so on. But this kind of love has to do with possession; it dehumanizes women and makes it impossible for a mature love relationship to develop. Furthermore, one usually loves a beautiful object only as long as it is beautiful. Once it ceases being attractive and comfortable a better one is available, and the first is discarded.

Sex-role stereotypes have also associated such traits as expressiveness, warmth, sensitivity, and emotionality with femininity. As we have already mentioned, these are characteristics that could be considered conducive to mature love. The trouble has been that too many social rules and constraints have tended to restrict these characteristics. For example, spontaneity, though it can be a positive feminine trait, may be discouraged within all but certain roles. Similarly, women have had to control their warmth, openness, and expressiveness especially in their contacts with men because such behaviors were often misinterpreted negatively. Unfortunately, it is the negative aspects of "femininity" that have been stressed, and these are obstacles to mature and mutually fulfilling love and sex relationships.

Myths about Love

In addition to all the obstacles that we have discussed in detail above, some myths about the nature and needs of men and women have tended to seriously interfere with the ability to achieve mature love. Some of these myths are related to and are a direct result of the social inequality that has always existed between men and women. The very myths that were meant to protect women and to provide them with economic, social, and legal security have often, in fact, psychologically short-changed them, in that they have traded love for security. Thus, while they were relatively assured of financial and social security, they often forfeited their chances for love.

ROMANTIC LOVE

The myth of romantic love, according to which one can really love another person only once in life, has been quite detrimental, particularly for women (Kooy, 1969), as we saw in

Chapter 1. Having loved one man, a woman may experience the desperate feeling that this may be her last chance for love; this belief has made many women even more dependent upon the man they loved. While a certain degree of emotional dependence is a necessary ingredient in love, the inability and unwillingness to consider potential alternative affective relationships can place a person at a disadvantage.

In an effort to protect women who occupied an inferior social position, monogamy was reinforced by a great number of legal and structural commitments. Thus, the only clear-cut and well-defined responsibility that men became conditioned to accept was the one derived from marriage. This artificially imposed sense of responsibility based on structural, legal, normative, and value constraints often replaced feelings of genuine, affective responsibility toward a wife. Men learned to be responsible toward a woman in the institutionalized relationship of marriage rather than toward the person they loved. Marriage became a "duty" that tied men to wives they no longer loved and to destructive relationships. Even when the marriage was in effect "dead" and they fell in love with another woman, many men were psychologically unable to make a genuine commitment to the woman they loved as long as they were married. And when they wanted to make such a commitment, they were made to feel uncomfortable, guilty, and dishonest. Although this condition has prevailed in order to discourage serious and disruptive dangers to marriage, in practice it has significantly contributed to the dehumanization of love.

Sweden is the only developed society that has made an effort to cope with the inhumanity involved in the legal and social separation of institutional responsibility from genuine affective responsibility (Abstract of Protocol on Justice Department, 1969). In that country people have long been free to love or to have sexual relations with another human being as long as they have been able and willing to carry out the social, humanitarian, and psychological responsibilities toward the other, regardless of whether or not a legal and structural responsibility was formally spelled out. Marital status is now fairly meaningless and devoid of legal status in Sweden because of the official and legal recognition of the fact that the relationships between people are important regardless of the extent of their institutionalization and legal endorsement (Safilios-Rothschild, 1974). Social responsibility is fulfilled in that clear legal responsibilities of both men and women have been spelled out toward their children, regardless of the type of relationship in which these children were conceived.

ETERNAL LOVE

Another myth about love that is typically Western and even more specifically American is one that relates to the possibility of maintaining love within a marriage. Today, people can look forward to a long life. And according to the myth, a marriage is supposed to last eternally. This "eternity" can be more than fifty years! Is this a feasible or a rational aim? Most people still marry at a fairly early age, and few are really prepared for the responsibilities involved in close living, early economic crises, childrearing — not to mention the search for maturity, identity, and individual growth. Love needs a great deal of time and energy and a good state of mind in order to grow and be kept alive. And the conventional married life rather infrequently offers this luxury. Given the problems of everyday living in a complex and ever-changing world, long-inefficient standards of male-female relationships, outmoded legal and social constraints, and the simple realities of people changing and developing in unique directions, it seems probable that we will have to take a closer look at this myth and explode it. The fact is, still, that love may be quite compatible with marriage, *if* we are willing to accept the fact that in most people's lives there will be more than one love and more than one marriage. A "real" love does not have to last eternally and a "good" marriage does not have to last a lifetime. It is the association of the quality of a relationship with its duration that is a myth to be debunked. A love may be "real," wonderful, and fulfilling for fifteen years—or five—but if it dies, this does not diminish its genuineness and beauty. A marriage may have been a great relationship that provided both people involved with enough freedom, warmth, and love for a certain time—but this is not to say that it will never become stale or destructive.

Good loves and marriages that end must not be viewed as failures. Unless we can shift our evaluation gears so that we are not influenced by the duration of a relationship in our judgment of its quality, love maintained in marriage will continue to be a frustrating myth that causes much unhappiness.

TOGETHERNESS

The development and maintenance of affectionate, self-actualizing love within the marital relationship has been made strenuous and often impossible because of another favorite American myth about love: that of togetherness.

According to this myth, people in love want to (and in a sense must) spend all their free time together. It is assumed that those in love share the same interests. If they do not, in the beginning, each learns how to like what the other likes, out of love. This behavior can be quite suffocating because it leaves little space for privacy and independence. In real life constraints surrounding the togetherness idea have been felt much more by women. Millions of loving American wives, for example, have forced themselves to watch football games because their husbands were fans; or have gone bowling with their husbands although they hated every minute of it. In some American marriages, particularly in the 50's and 60's, the husbands have wanted or even demanded that their wives be available and willing to join them in their activities, hobbies and pastimes. And they considered this an indication of love. Many women have never developed their own interests and talents because they were afraid that this separateness would interfere with the love relationship they had with their busbands. Sadly, the opposite often occurred. The togetherness suppressed growth and brought about boredom that tended to dull the feelings. The devastating effects of togetherness upon love relationships within a marriage become sharper within the long duration of marriage in the U.S.

FIDELITY

According to the fidelity myth, people in love — particularly married people — must stay faithful to each other or their love will suffer and eventually die. Faithfulness has most often been broadly defined so as to preclude most types of other close relationships undertaken independently of the partner. In this way, close relationships with opposite-sex colleagues and friends have been suspect because of the underlying sexual potential. These exclusivity rules often made love and marriage suffocating and deprived people of rich and rewarding relationships. When there is a requirement that the love relationship must satisfy *all* needs for diversity, for companionship, and for understanding, love becomes stifled.

Interestingly enough, within American society a sexual-love infidelity has been considered more serious and threatening than an intellectual-love infidelity. The opposite has been found to be true within the French society (*Patterns of Sex and Love,* 1961). Actually, there is some evidence that some American wives have not only tolerated but even welcomed some of the social and supportive roles played by their husbands' secretaries and/or assistants, as long as they were reasonably sure that there was no sexual relationship (Cuber and Harroff, 1968; Mulligan, 1972). In fact, among upper- and upper-middle-class couples the often crucial role of a secretary or assistant is institutionalized into an "office wife" role with a variety of diffuse components that may or may not also include the sexual component (Peterson, 1971; Mulligan, 1972).

Recent evidence from studies of unfaithful marriage partners as well as from "swinging" couples supports the idea that for many people the stringent norm of fidelity may be a myth. In some cases spouses claim that sexual infidelities, instead of being disruptive, tend to revive and improve the love relationship between them, as long as these infidelities remain predominantly sexual and are clearly defined as short-lived, transient, and secondary to the main relationship (Bartell, 1971; Boylan, 1971; Myer and Liggit, 1972; Ziskin and Ziskin, 1973). Couples who live together in nonexclusive relationships claim that they are able to love each other while they have casual sexual relations with others (Huang, 1974). The important new element is the fact that the extramarital sexual relationships are not secret; the one spouse is not "cheating" on the other. In the new "open" marriages, spouses are free to experience and enjoy intimate relationships with friends of the other sex, which may or may not involve sexual relations, without feeling that these *additional* relationships must replace the marital relationship. Mature spouses who love each other are supposed to be able to bring back to their marriage and share with their partner the love, intimacy, and growth that they have gained through these additional relationships, thus extending the marital relationship and making it richer and even more intimate (O'Neill and O'Neill, 1972). This of course represents a new ideal, which may be realized by some unusually mature loving couples, but it is still difficult to tell to what extent or how fast such a pattern could be adopted by the majority of people.

Is Love Possible between Unequals?

Traditionally, men and women have been socially unequal, the women occupying a more or less clearly demarcated inferior social position. This social inequality persists today despite current liberation movements and ideologies. A very basic question that has been often raised in recent years is whether or not people who are socially unequal can love each other. Some claim that love is only possible between relatively equal people who can have equally high esteem for each other (Greer, 1971; Kasten, 1972; Morell, 1973). Here the definition of love becomes crucial. Some kind of love may exist between equal as well as between very unequal people, but the type of love possible in the two contexts is radically different. Love between unequals tends to encourage the objectification that we have discussed earlier — a man is apt to see a woman as a valuable object to possess, and a woman may regard a man as an object to "catch" by the use of feminine wiles. Love between two people who perceive one another to be on a fairly equal basis has more chance of being a mature relationship between two human beings.

When men and women are socially unequal, it is often difficult to develop love relationships partly because, as we saw earlier, masculine and feminine sex-role stereotypes are fairly incompatible with the very essence of a loving *human* relationship. Social inequality implies a set of very different social structural conditions, options, and opportunities for men and women that do not allow either freely to choose and love. Those in the inferior social position — the women — must strive to improve their status, even at the cost of foregoing love and the enjoyment of sexuality. Their very social and psychological identity depends upon men's approval, interest, and love (Kasten, 1972). This precarious source of identity controlled by men rather than by themselves makes women anxious to please and to serve men but at the same time to resent them and to scheme and plot to secure their interest, love, and protection (Morell, 1973). What conditions can be more dehumanizing for love, for either sex?

In societies clearly and rigidly stratified on the basis of sex, men have had to show their masculinity and superiority by dominating their girlfriends and wives and by maintaining a facade of strength and invulnerability. They have had not only the obligation but the compulsion to control all situations, to dominate, and to be powerful, never being able to relax or to relinquish their superordinate position. They could not afford to show weakness, dependence, fear; thus, to admit love has been forbidden, an admission of loss of control. This type of masculine iron shield has most often interfered with the establishment of close, intimate relationships.

Husbands could still "love" their wives as prized possessions. They could desire them sexually; they could want to own them and protect them; they cared about their welfare; and they could be very unhappy if they lost them. But this is a limited definition of love; it does not necessarily entail a close, intimate relationship. On the side of women, their awareness of their inferior social status and opportunities have rendered them so dependent upon men and so alienated that many of them are convinced that love is less important than financial and status considerations. Some studies have clearly illustrated how women can "talk themselves into loving" a man who is "Mr. Right" in terms of social characteristics, even when they were initially indifferent (Kephart, 1967; Hochschild, 1975). Women, more than men, seem to develop the ability to analyze and manipulate their feelings so that what they *ought* to do is chosen over what they want to do (Hochschild, 1975). This ability to mold and redirect feelings according to their appropriateness allows women to make the "right" decisions about marriage rather than to be swept away by their emotions. The social and economic penalties for letting their feelings develop freely and spontaneously could be too high for women to indulge in such a luxury.

Furthermore, women less often than men end up by marrying the person they love. In the case of men their own love feelings tend to determine their marital choice more than their partner's feelings. In the case of women the contrary trend has been true: the intensity of the future husband's love feelings carries more weight than their own feelings. There is research evidence that the type of love asymmetry in which the husband is perceived (by both spouses) as the most loving of the two is at least twice as frequent as the reverse asymmetry (Broderick and Hicks, 1970; Safilios-Rothschild, 1976). This situation has been facilitated by means of two equally important mechanisms. First, since men have traditionally initiated and determined marriage and other sexual and affective relationships, they have had a greater chance than women to marry the person they loved. Women, who had to wait passively for Prince Charming, usually could not take the chance to refuse the marriage proposal of a socially desirable man whom they did not love (especially if he was not entirely unattractive) because of uncertainty — what if the "great love" never came along? Second, men could more often than women afford to marry the woman they loved, even when she was of lower social class than themselves, because the family's financial and social status has been determined by men. Women, on the other hand, have been conditioned to look for men of at least equal or higher status. So they had to marry the "right" man, even if they did not love him. The ability to manipulate emotions and love and partially to convince themselves that they "loved" the right man has softened hard reality.

In general, it seems that in societies in which men and women have had unequal opportunities, social status, and access to money, it is difficult to marry strictly for love. Even when this occurs, it is hard to establish and maintain an intimate, open, honest love relationship that is without power and domination hangups and allows the couple to grow as individual people.

Psychoanalysts and psychologists tell us that as long as there is social inequality between men and women, and women are defined as being not only different but also less significant, it is natural for both men and women to want to associate with and be liked and approved by the important people — the men (Seidenberg, 1972; Miller, 1972; Lipman-Blumen, 1976). This explains why men have always sought and preferred the company of other men, especially men whom they admired for their accomplishments or personality. Men's important reference group has always been other men. Lipman-Blumen (1976) postulates that probably the somewhat exaggerated fear of male homosexuality is based on the fact that boys and later men are usually more interested in each other than they are in girls and women. Because society has had to check homosexuality in order to assure the survival of the human race, a paradox has been created in that, while men are primarily attracted to each other, their relationships are often thwarted and restricted by stringent taboos. In their relationships with other men they are not allowed to express feelings and emotions, such as affection or weakness, and cannot, therefore, relate at any emotional depth and experience emotional closeness with other men (Goldberg, 1976). They are restricted to the acceptable masculine mode of association: competing with each other at work, sports, or games—in this way trying to gain each other's approval and admiration (Miller, 1972). Despite these restrictions on self-disclosure and emotional expression, men have been able to satisfy their needs for acceptance, companionship, friendship, intellectual stimulation, and fun through these relationships with other men (Lipman-Blumen, 1976). Their sexual needs, however, have traditionally had to be satisfied through women, despite the fact that women were considered inferior and insignificant.* Because men have been put in the situation of being dependent solely on women for the expression and satisfaction of their sexual needs, they often end by despising not only the women who have sexual "power" over them but also themselves for their "weakness"—their vulnerability vis-à-vis their "social inferiors." Of course, because men have access to social power, they have been able to develop a number of mechanisms to establish norms and values that have helped decrease their sexual vulnerability. They have been more or less able to regulate women's sexual behavior; to determine the timing and nature of sexual encounters; and to maximize their chances for obtaining the sexual partner they want in exchange for marriage and/or money, status, or power. Of course, these

---

*In some cultures such as Mediterranean, Arab, and Latin American societies, men have been allowed a much greater latitude in their expression of affection for each other (in terms of touching, hugging, and even kissing) as well as in their expression of weakness, sorrow, admiration, and friendly mutual love and concern. Because in these societies male friendships can and often do achieve considerable emotional depth, men need women only to fulfill their sexual needs, and mature love between men and women has often been in these cases even more elusive than in other societies.

mechanisms do not always work. As women have started to gain a few rights, some of them, when sexually desired by men, utilize their sexual power in order to manipulate men or flatly refuse to have anything to do with them no matter how attractive the offer. In traditional settings, men have taken a woman's refusal as a serious affront and have sometimes resorted to violence (killing her or beating her up) or to a type of psychological blackmail that allowed them to regain the dominant, powerful position. A striking example of the second alternative is the kidnapping and raping of unwilling women in Sicily and rural Greece in order to force them to accept marriage to avoid the very powerful stigma of dishonor.

Under these conditions, the possibility of a real love relationship developing between a woman and a man is understandably elusive. Women have had to attract men sexually because otherwise they would not have access to money, status, power, or the possibility of associating with the important and interesting people in society. They have had, therefore, to fashion themselves as attractive sex objects in whatever style they felt would make them most desirable to men; and they have been conditioned to sell their unique commodity to the highest bidder (Lipman-Blumen, 1976). But once reduced to a sex object, can a woman still love as a human being? Can she allow her desires and personality to be freely expressed, thus taking the chance of displeasing men? Can she ask for her needs to be satisfied when she often has to compete with her lover's or husband's male friends and colleagues for his time, attention, and interest? And on the side of men, since sexuality is something that "socially inferior" women can offer, is it possible for men to love a sexually desirable woman in any other way but as an object to be used, possessed, even needed, but never loved for her intrinsic value? It is striking to note that traditional men have often reserved feelings of love for those women whose sexuality is secondary, unattainable, or entirely tabooed. They may love their mothers, their sisters, the mothers of their children, to whom they are very little if at all sexually attracted, or women who for a variety of social obstacles are sexually unattainable. Even today some men tend to divide women into two categories: those whom they consider as exciting sexual partners for brief encounters but whom they would never love; and those whom they define as interesting, stimulating companions, the sexual attraction playing only a marginal role. Love is reserved for the second category of women, whom they consider more as equals. Some of the "liberated" men of our time still have problems in fully integrating sexuality as an important component in their love relationships with women they admire and consider on an equal basis. Somehow an unspoken belief persists that the sexual desirability of a woman in some way degrades her and diminishes her human worth and dignity!

Because women have been viewed as the "second-best" for men and a necessary evil, men have tried to reconcile their resentment at having to love and express their sexuality with a socially inferior being by idealizing the woman they loved (Firestone, 1970). In order to feel more comfortable about desiring and wanting to associate with a social inferior, men have tended to attribute to the desirable woman admirable qualities and characteristics that made her stand apart from other women. There are some indications that unless men can by some mechanism elevate in their own eyes a woman from her socially inferior status to that of a friend and companion (a status reserved to social equals), they cannot love women as human beings. This tendency explains why even in traditional societies husbands who very much love their wives (more than they are loved in return) are willing to share the family power with them (Safilios-Rothschild, 1976). Probably because of this "elevating" function, some men have tended to be more attracted to women desired and loved by other men. The attraction toward a woman in fact is apt to be greater the more successful and important are the men who love her.

A man's desire and love for a woman has traditionally had to be quite strong and overwhelming before it could compete with the feelings for a man's close male friends. Women have in many cases had to compete with a man's friends for his attention even harder than they had to compete with other attractive women. It is not uncommon for a woman to feel convinced of a man's love when he wants to spend more time with her than with his male friends. Another proof of love is acknowledged when the man no longer discusses his woman or their relationship with his close friends for approval. As long as a man discusses his relationship with his male friends, these friends are in fact given the right to analyze, criticize, and eventually approve or disapprove of the woman. Once this discussion is discontinued, the woman is given more leeway to influence the man and to determine the outcome of the relationship.

We have discussed whether or not mature love is possible given the unequal status of men and women; we can also ask the same question about the sexual relationship. As we have seen, in traditional societies the sex-role stereotypes seriously interfere with the quality of sexual relations. For a different set of reasons, both men and women have typically been sexually dissatisfied and frustrated. Men have been compelled to feel like sex machines and thus have not known how to improve the quality of the sexual relationship with any particular partner. Such an improvement requires sensitivity, understanding of the woman's needs, as well as her own full development of her sexuality and her active sexual role. All these necessary conditions have been incompatible with sex-role stereotypes. In traditional societies women have seldom been able to discover their sexual potential and often have not dared even express their sexual needs or pleasures. In addition, women's inferior social position has made them particularly vulnerable to sexual exploitation by powerful men, thus depriving them of their sole marketable asset: their virginity. All this results in dehumanization and alienation of sex for both men and women. Only social equality can allow women to enjoy their sexuality and thus to also decrease men's sexual frustrations (Coleman, 1966).

Interestingly, occasionally men have been able to relax much more in their relationships with prostitutes and mistresses.

Within the context of these relationships, they did not feel the constant need to dominate and could enjoy receiving attention, sexual activity, and learning sexual and/or social skills without fearing a threat to their masculinity and a loss of power. They have also often felt freer to talk openly about their preoccupations, fears, and weaknesses, and to bare their souls in a way that they seldom did with their wives or marriageable girlfriends. Thus, in these socially "unacceptable" relationships outside marriage, men have been able to abandon their dominant and tough masculine role, probably because the structural conditions inherent in these relationships usually made it impossible for the women involved to dominate them. Actually, partly because men have sometimes had as mistresses women who were more their social equals than were their wives, and partly because they felt less constrained in a nonmarital situation, their relationships with such women have often been "true" love relationships. Many men whose wives play the traditional role of wife and mother have fallen in love with a successful career woman who was their social equal. Because in these extramarital love relationships men often let their "masculine" defenses down, these "other" women have sometimes been able to effectively manipulate them.

Today, as men continue to move toward being less influenced by masculine stereotypes, they increasingly allow themselves to love and feel less anxious about being vulnerable and dependent upon women. As sex-role stereotypes lose their grip on people and the sexual double standard subsides, men and women tend to redefine love and to have much higher expectations about what love must represent in their lives. This redefinition involves a combination of personal freedom, continuous growth, closeness, intimacy, openness, and honesty, as well as tenderness, exclusivity, and sexual satisfaction. Within the context of this type of love, there is no place for domination, power, and indifference games. Instead, each person feels comfortable in alternating from a dominant to a subordinate proposition from situation to situation and from time to time. This type of "total" love-sex relationship remains an ideal difficult to achieve at present except for limited time periods, and most often outside marriage and parenthood. This difficulty stems partly from the fact that we have not been socialized to sustain such equal, loving relationships (Seidenberg, 1972) and partly because the routine tasks and everyday stress of married life and particularly of parenthood often represent insurmountable structural obstacles to the maintenance of such a delicate and demanding love relationship. It takes exceptional people who are willing to work through all kinds of complexes, selfish concerns and preoccupations, childhood habits, as well as structural strains and stresses in order to learn how to make love a source of happiness, self- and other-actualization, continuous growth, and excitement. Liberation from sex-role stereotypes is a necessary but not a sufficient condition for achieving this type of love relationship. It is possible that our present socialization, experiences, and long-term relationships block us from seeing what conditions and behaviors facilitate or are basic to living this type of ideal love that many of us may never experience.

Some of the same obstacles to the development of love also interfere with men's and women's ability to develop and enjoy friendships and work relationships. In Chapter 5, we shall see how the stereotypic notions of masculinity and femininity in particular push men and women to subvert all types of relationships to sexual.

Five

STRANGERS,
FRIENDS, AND COLLEAGUES

Sexuality is claimed to be an important element in all human relationships—even in friendships between members of the same sex and relationships between close relatives. This may be true if sexuality is broadly defined to include sensuality and underlying sexual feelings that are not normally translated into behavior or even acknowledged consciously. In close kinship relations such as those between a brother and sister, a father and daughter (or step-daughter), a mother and son (or step-son), a man and his mother-in-law, or a man and his sister-in-law, sexual behavior is strictly tabooed—it is considered a major social transgression that may be seriously punished. Furthermore, such a transgression is supposed to indicate the existence of psychological problems or lead to serious psychological problems if imposed on innocent and/or immature partners. Homosexuality traditionally has been tabooed in Western cultures and in many societies it has been (and is) punished as a crime; in others it has been treated as a mental illness. In our society this has affected the behavior of men and women within close relationships. Men, in particular, because of the rigid stereotypes that have defined their masculinity and because of the fear of loss of control and power, have been allowed less emotional closeness to other men than have women in close same-sex friendships. In relating to close male friends (unless interested and willing to risk the stigma and price of homosexuality), men have had to continuously emphasize their heterosexuality as well as their masculinity. This preoccupation often marked men's friendships with other men with a certain lack of expressed emotions and feelings.* Moreover, it meant that their relations with women *had* to be *sexual.*

Because the potentially underlying sexuality between close family members or members of the same sex in practically all societies has been in some way stigmatized and/or punished, special elements are introduced in the relationships. These complexities merit detailed discussion, and we will not deal with them here. Instead, the focus will be on the different types of relationships between adult men and women that are initially established for other purposes than sex or love. There is, however, always the potential that these relationships may lead to sexual attraction and/or love. Every time a man and a woman meet, their socialization has already conditioned them to evaluate each other with regard to sexual attractiveness on the basis of a number of visible cues, physical as well as social (Pankin, 1973). Because this evaluation process takes place almost automatically, the potential is there whether or not it is consciously recognized or acted upon. These relationships may vary from chance encounters between strangers to work relationships with colleagues and fellow-workers, to acquaintances and different types of friendships.

*As we already saw in Chapter 4, Latin and Mediterranean men have been allowed a considerable latitude in expressing feelings and emotions toward close friends. But probably because they have been allowed to express their feelings, they also had to avert any suspicion of homosexuality by a continuous and almost compulsive preoccupation with the conquest of women. Women, on the other hand, usually have been able to enjoy more intimacy and expression of feelings with close friends without being suspected of lesbianism.

Encounters with Strangers

Some encounters with strangers of the opposite sex are truly "incidental" in that no effort has been made to initiate them. They take place while people are going about their normal activities and lives. When, however, people *want* to meet other people, they may incorporate into their everyday living patterns and activities that are conducive to meeting new people. Divorced or single people, for example, may join sports or social clubs and associations or move to apartment complexes in which many (or all) people are single. In this case, encounters with strangers are "purposeful" but the circumstances are such that the involved people seem to have a primary purpose other than meeting new people. One is able to claim that the only reason he has joined the tennis club is because he enjoys playing tennis. Finally, there are encounters with strangers that are deliberately planned for that one reason alone. Going to singles bars, discotheques where single people meet, or trips for singles — all are aimed *specifically* at meeting other people. These clearly "purposeful" encounters with strangers are engineered in order to start sexual and love relationships and will not, therefore, be dealt with here. We shall only discuss the different types of "incidental" encounters, for which the rules, expectations, and outcomes are vague and undefined.

Actually, men and women have many chances to interact with strangers in the normal course of their lives. Housewives with small children are the major exception — they usually have few chances to meet male strangers. Men, on the other hand, and working women normally have many more opportunities to incidentally meet strangers. The higher the education and occupational status, the greater the range of opportunities for different types of encounters with strangers in a variety of settings. The travel dimension built into most middle-class male occupations multiplies such chance encounters — especially in planes between two dry martinis. Who are the women they meet? Professional women, college students, women on vacations, stewardesses, rental car agents, airline ground personnel, and cocktail lounge and restaurant waitresses. Sitting next to each other in a plane is one type of encounter between strangers in which it is almost as acceptable for women as it is for men to initiate the conversation around some ritualized occurrence.

Usually, strangers who would like to start talking to each other provide encouraging nonverbal cues. But sometimes one of the two, most often the man, is outgoing and/or interested enough to start the conversation without waiting for the right cues or even in the presence of unfavorable cues. Actually, men tend to be insensitive to negative cues from a woman stranger. For example, a woman working while on a plane may not encourage communication with a man, but he may pursue her, not believing that she can be serious about her work. If she is there alone, the male reasoning goes, she is expected to welcome male attention and conversation (Pogrebin, 1975), and therefore, her resistance or reluctance is often viewed as playful rather than real.

Sometimes the motivation for striking a conversation may be solely for information — for example, concerning the city to which one is flying. Even when this continues to other subjects, it can remain at a superficial informational level, devoid of any other overtones. At other times, the conversation starts because one finds the other attractive and *simpatico,* this attraction being vague and undefined. Most often men's apparent social status and women's attractiveness determine whether or not two strangers will be attracted to each other (Davis, 1973). Occasionally, however, strangers may want to start talking to each other because the other looks exotic or intriguing and the basis for the attraction may be curiosity or amusement rather than a more conventional reason. In some cases, after a few sentences have been exchanged it becomes abundantly clear to one or both that the initial diffuse attraction was wrong. The additional information that comes through concerning the stranger's intelligence or attitudes may be such that it turns the other completely off so that he or she discourages the continuation of the conversation. But when the initial attraction is reinforced, there is a tendency toward increasingly more intimate exchanges of information, values, ideas, and even feelings. This does not necessarily mean that the encounter is intended to be continued in some kind of friendship, or sexual relationship. Most often people enjoy this conversational intimacy exactly *because* they are strangers and the probability for any kind of continuity is rather small. In fact, sometimes people can feel more at ease in revealing personal, intimate information to strangers than to friends. The limited duration of the encounter gives the participants "a feeling of unaccountability and invulnerability which can have the effect of increasing openness" (Rubin, 1974). In the process of this conversation they can learn how men (or women) feel about or react to a particular behavior by asking directly or by trying out without penalty different types of "routines," behaviors, and facades. Such encounters offer the opportunity to learn about the other sex by trying out behaviors or by making overtures with a minimum risk of rejection, since it is quite easy to turn around and claim that overtures or proposals were not seriously meant (Pankin, 1973).

Sometimes both strangers clearly and openly recognize and admit that they have no interest in further pursuing an encounter, but that they enjoy talking with each other and thus learning more about themselves as well as about others. At other times, all doors are left open to all possibilities and one or both carefully (or less carefully) feel their way toward these possibilities. An important condition for continuation is of course that the horizon is clear in terms of commitments and relationships to other people, unless they are both interested in a brief sexual adventure.

While the probability is small that a brief encounter between a man and a woman as strangers will lead to a friendship or to a sexual or love relationship, it must be recognized that such encounters in fact represent a frequent and important type of beginning for short- and long-term relationships. It is only because of the great frequency of such encounters between strangers that the probability of any one such meeting having any kind of continuity is small. One of the reasons why this is so is the fact that the opportunity for misrepresentation is high, since in chance meetings the strangers have little information about each other than what is volunteered.* A married person can present him/herself as single and a salesperson, as an executive. This lack of valid relevant information makes women in particular hesitant to encourage continuity, even when the attraction is high. In general, continuity whenever it happens is easier in the form of friendship or a casual sexual relationship without any commitment than in the form of a love relationship. This is so because often the attracted strangers already have other love commitments, or because what attracted them in a superficial encounter is not necessarily what counts for them in a love relationship (Davis, 1973).

But whatever the level of interest or awareness of interest in some kind of continuity, brief encounters with strangers can be rewarding and pleasant. They are an important way to test oneself in a social situation and to validate one's style of relating with the other sex. A pleasant encounter with a stranger can help gain that extra insight and self-confidence that one needs in order to cope with sexual and love relationships. Being liked, appreciated, and admired is flattering and a boost to one's morale, even when the encounter has no continuity. And the admiration received is even more flattering when directed to one's personality and outlook on life rather than solely to looks (in the case of women) or achievements (in the case of men). The learning aspect in such meetings involves a variety of messages related to the roles of men and women, the nature and variety of man-woman relationships, sexuality, marriage, love, and coping with

*When chance encounters occur within the context of athletic clubs or the swimming pool of an apartment house, the strangers either may already have some information about each other or they can easily have access to such information (Davis, 1973).

emotions and failures. Men, for example, may be exposed for the first time to successful, independent, and attractive women, an experience that may challenge their stereotypic view of women and help them reconsider the validity of these stereotypes. This may help them in future opportunities to relate somewhat differently to women—that is, not entirely or primarily in terms of their physical attractiveness but also in terms of who they are as people and what they have to say.

But occasionally, the insights and learning that takes place in encounters with strangers may be painful and bitter. Women may, for example, learn that some very intelligent and attractive men can relate to women only sexually, and see women as inferior, unimportant beings. This message is all the more painful because such men are potentially interesting but are apt to be excluded from the "possibilities" by the more liberated woman.

Whatever the content, nature and outcome of chance meetings between strangers, these encounters can be important in acquiring self- and other-knowledge. They may in fact represent helpful socialization experiences for the establishment of fulfilling friendships between men and women. Possibly, such meetings can help us overcome some of the stereotyped and destructive patterns that up to now have characterized men-women relationships. Hopefully, we can eventually learn how to cope with attraction and sensuality in the context of friendship so as to enrich the relationship rather than subvert it to a sexual one.

Working Together

Work has traditionally been a masculine domain. Whenever women were allowed to enter it, they did so either under the supervision of a male member of the family or another man or they worked exclusively with other women. Even at present in most traditional societies women who work usually do so at home, or in settings in which only women work, or under the direct supervision of a male family member. Some typical "feminine" occupations are maids, dressmakers, hairdressers, midwives, elementary and nursery school teachers, and among physicians, pediatricians or gynecologists — that is, occupations which can be practiced at home or which put them primarily in contact with women clients or children. Women are also actively involved in agriculture in most of the Third-World countries (Safilios-Rothschild, 1975), where they either work together with other women relatives or under the direction of male members of the family. In some Muslim countries, such as Pakistan, the avoidance of work-related contacts between men and women has been carried to an extreme; women are not allowed to be the clients of male physicians, lawyers, teachers, professors, bank clerks, or family planning workers. Women have been trained to serve only women clients (Safilios-Rothschild, 1972).

The rationale for this work-sex segregation has been the fear that women's morality might be compromised by a close contact with men. The assumptions here are clear. When men come into "close" contact with women, they become sexually interested in them (unless they are too old or ugly), since the only way in which men can relate to women is sexually. Women, on the other hand, cannot resist or are afraid to reject men's sexual proposals. The fear element is valid — men have been known to punish women, predominantly subordinate in the work hierarchy, for having rejected their sexual proposals by firing them, depriving them of due promotions, or by starting a painful cold war. But the implication remains that women, regardless of the fear element, are not able to resist men, an implication that shows the ambivalent image that women have had in traditional societies as dehumanized objects that are variously sexual and sexless.

Because in traditional societies low-income women are most often forced by economic necessity to work in jobs together with men, such as in factories, and to occupy the lowest positions, they are quite vulnerable to sexual exploitation. They cannot risk losing their jobs because their family's survival depends on them — and many submit to sexual exploitation by their male bosses because of this. By this process some occupations become stigmatized as inappropriate for "proper" women. In India, for example, the occupation of nursing is considered unsuitable for women because of the necessary intimate contacts with men patients and the entry of low-social-status women who have little bargaining position vis-à-vis male physicians or patients (Rajogopalan, 1963).

In nontraditional societies in which more women have moved into a relatively wider range of occupations, the segregation between men and women at work is still maintained to a considerable degree by means of different types of mechanisms. In some work settings, women are placed in job classifications designed as "feminine" — and are often spatially segregated from the "masculine" job classifications. Very often the work that men and women do in corresponding job classifications is the same, or at least the skills required for the job are the same, but the segregation on the basis of gender makes working women more acceptable to men. Women can in this way be "kept in their place" spatially, psychologically, and occupationally; they can be paid less and not promoted as frequently as men in corresponding "masculine" jobs. But probably the most important function of sex segregation at work is that it is said to minimize conflict and disruption because of sexual attraction and rivalries. Men can maintain the all-male in-group at work and their solidarity is not disrupted by sexual competition and jealousy. Since very few men know how to deal with women as colleagues and co-workers, they feel more comfortable when the sexual and the occupational spheres are neatly separated. This separateness created through the subordination of women in the workworld is also evident in the fact that women have been discouraged from becoming physicians, lawyers, dentists, architects, or professors (except in nursing, home economics, or social work where the majority of students have been women). In this way, men never found themselves in the disadvantaged subordinate position of patient, student, or client. The pattern of all-male professions in these occupations also precluded the possibility of men being sexually propositioned and thus threatened or exploited by women professionals in positions of power.

Whenever total spatial and occupational sex segregation is not possible, a certain separateness through subordination is achieved by assigning women to low-level auxiliary positions in which they must help men carry out their important functions. Women are secretaries and assistants to men. Women are clerks and men are supervisors. This type of occupational sex segregation, while it still keeps women "in their place," does not preclude extensive contacts between men and women within the work settings. But since men are most often in superior positions, these work contacts are usually between unequals. In this way, even when men become emotionally and/or sexually involved with women, they can maintain considerable control over such relationships by the mere fact that they can use their work-related power. The sexual and affective potentials involved in these contacts are well-documented in the number of men who marry as their first or second wife their secretary or assistant, and by the much larger number of men who have sexual and/or love relationships with their female subordinates. In some cases, in fact, there is some evidence that such a relationship may be the meaningful one in the man's life who for a variety of social, psychological, and financial reasons does not divorce his wife (Cuber and Harroff, 1966; Peterson, 1971).

Even more frequent than actual sexual and love relationships are feelings of attraction or even a strong emotional commitment for a work associate which may never be translated into a sexual or love relationship. In fact, such an emotional commitment may sometimes remain entirely private in that it is not communicated (at least verbally) to the person concerned. But it is usually quite influential, occasionally even more so than an actual relationship (Zetterberg, 1966). Often the women who are the objects of such strong emotional feelings can successfully manipulate male bosses or co-workers (Zetterberg, 1966; Aronson and Aronson, 1971). And their manipulative power has been found to be even greater when the men attracted to them are *not* having a sexual relationship with them. Some women are quite conscious of the greater power potential of sexual or emotional attraction over an actual relationship, and consequently they try to maintain and utilize the existing sexual tensions as long as possible (Pogrebin, 1975).

The presence of emotional overtones and attraction of varying intensity between women and men in different work and authority positions need not necessarily affect or in any way interfere with work relationships. But as the situation currently stands in our society, they often do interfere and have a disruptive effect. Because of the existing male-female inequalities, some men are especially vulnerable to manipulation, and some women have chosen to capitalize upon their "sexual power." It is easy to justify the use of attractiveness and potential sexuality in the interest of diminishing the inequality gap between men and women. As long as women are generally seen as being less competent and serious workers than men, the level of their performance will not be a sufficient or decisive factor in their work career. As long as men evaluate women workers more on the basis of their attractiveness than on the basis of their work ability and performance, they will leave themselves open to the possibility of manipulation by women who seek to use their only source of power and control. It is only when there is no occupational discrimination on the basis of gender that we can expect men and women to enjoy existing attractions without using them in power and vengeance games.

Actually, one of the reasons for which men have objected to women entering masculine occupations as equal co-workers has been their fear that women may tend to be treated preferentially because of their attractiveness and sexual potential (e.g., *Policewomen on Patrol*, 1973). This favoritism may be feared both because of ongoing sexual or love relationships between men superiors and women subordinates or because of existing sexual attraction or emotional "weaknesses" on the part of bosses and co-workers. Furthermore, because of the emotional and sexual complications when men and women are found in the same occupational setting as either equal or unequal co-workers, wives have traditionally resented and fought against other women's entry into masculine occupations. Actually, these kinds of fears and objections have often acted as an additional powerful barrier to women's occupational integration. Recently, wives complained bitterly and vociferously when police departments decided to hire policewomen and to allow them to go on regular patrol duty as partners with men. In one recent study, about half of the married policemen believed that their wives would be strongly opposed to their having a woman patrol partner (*Policewomen on Patrol,* 1973). Similarly, in the Navy women have not been allowed to go on sea duty in the same boat with men over several months partly because of the fear that sexual and love relationships might take place across ranks and that this would create discipline and functioning problems; and partly because there is the feeling that extramarital relations might be encouraged. In addition, Navy wives have protested vehemently against such a possibility; they feel it would represent a more tangible threat to marital stability than do the women (most often prostitutes) their husbands briefly meet in harbors (Charlton, 1972).

Wives' fears are intensified by the fact that husbands (and men in general) have traditionally preferred to hire attractive over unattractive women, sometimes even at the price of competency. This may have been partially due to a universal human preference for associating with attractive people, but probably more important is men's tendency to relate to all women at the sexual level, as potential sexual partners. This preference has heavily influenced the type of interaction possible between work associates. Women learned that they could use their attractiveness to manipulate men. Men in power positions, on the other hand, learned that they could flirt, flatter, and treat women co-workers and subordinates as dates instead of giving them salary raises or promotions for work dedication or outstanding work performance (Acker and Van Houten, 1974). Attractiveness underlines the sex-object image of women and interferes with their ability to be taken seriously at work and to be considered and rewarded as competent workers (Prather, 1971; Smith, 1972). And, despite the fact that women tried to cash in on their attractiveness "to get ahead," because of their powerlessness and inferior social status, they often ended by being doubly exploited by male superiors: sexually and occupationally.

As increasingly more women enter the labor force, men will no longer be able to screen out unattractive qualified women. Some will be average and some homely. Some will have pleasant, appealing personalities and others will be more difficult people. In this way, the image of working women will be "normalized" to include a wide range of types and appearances, as is true for men. This can be expected to have important consequences for the nature of work relationships between men and women. Women workers may come to be seen less as sex objects and men may learn to relate to them in terms of work contributions, quality of performance, ideas, and creativity, as well as in terms of sexuality (Safilios-Rothschild, 1977). This "normalization," therefore, can be expected to promote more mature and equitable relationships between men and women in the working setting. Furthermore, the fact that women will increasingly have the power to hire and promote men subordinates will have an effect. If, during the transition, some are tempted to favor or sexually exploit attractive men, this may help make men aware of the discomfort women have undergone in the past. It is possible that this awareness may help eventually diminish exploitation and the objectification of men and women.

Clearly, many of the interpersonal strains between men and women in the work setting come from the fact that women have been hired in many circumstances on the basis of their attractiveness rather than their competence; and from men's and women's inability to view each other as human beings of equal worth who have much more to offer each other than sex or sexually based love.

There are indications that working men and women are slowly learning to be colleagues and friends rather than manipulable objects. Slowly, people are learning to enjoy the company and conversation of the opposite sex without feeling compelled to relate to one another sexually. Working women appear to be learning how to cope with male subordinates or equals, especially when these men are attractive. They are becoming resocialized so as not to feel that they *must* please the men with whom they work (equals, subordinates, or bosses). Many women in the workworld today are refusing to be sex objects. This means that their primary concern is not orienting their behavior and looks to manipulating men through sexual attraction. It means that they are behaving in a way that will cause others — men and women — to perceive them as competent workers and whole human beings. They, furthermore, learn how to accept but not be in any way influenced by men's flattery, flirting, and sexual propositioning (Pogrebin, 1975).

An important question remains necessarily unanswered until men and women have really learned to become friends and colleagues and to value these relationships as much as sexual and love relationships. Is a good work relationship between a man and a woman the kind of relationship that is conducive to the most satisfactory love relationship? Is it "natural" for two people who have a close and successful work relationship to fall in love and possibly marry? And if so, what are the implications for the family in the present and immediate future? In other societies in which it is not unusual for both husband and wife to work, it is typical for people to marry much later than in the United States. Also, the most usual pattern is for both spouses to have the same occupation and to work in the same work setting. It may be that a close working relationship has a high probability of breeding intimacy, admiration, attraction, and love — possibly a good working relationship may be the best basis for marriage.

On Being Friends

Within the context of the American society, men and women have been provided with hardly any socialization experiences that prepare them for being good friends with each other. From very early adolescence, when girls and boys for the first time become interested in associating with each other, they are pressured to date and to think in terms of romance. There is no institutionalized alternative that allows them to consider friendship without romantic overtones. This is a serious socialization handicap, and it has long-range consequences for the possible man-woman relationships.

There is evidence that in some societies, boys and girls learn how to value friendship sometimes even more than sexual and love relationships. In urban Greece, for example, as well as in other Mediterranean societies, middle- and upper-middle-class boys and girls enjoy the institution of *parea* from the time they are 15 or 16 years old. *Parea* usually replaces or supplements dating (which is exclusive rather than multiple) and is composed of a number of boys and girls whose pairing is taboo. *Parea* members go out together socially, spend hours talking and playing together and learn to associate with peers of both sexes and to enjoy them as friends and persons rather than as dates (Safilios-Rothschild, 1975b). The crucial socialization function of *parea* is evident in the adult men's and women's ability to have and enjoy friendships with both sexes and a *parea* throughout life, in addition to sexual, love, and marital relationships.

It must be noted, however, that despite the fact that *parea* members are not supposed to develop romantic interest in each other, occasionally this happens. The pair then either drops from the *parea* or maintains the friendship appearance within the context of the *parea*, while at the same time dating each other outside of it.

There are some sporadic reports that at least some teenagers and young people have started going out in groups without any special pairing arrangement. Although no systematic research data are available, to the extent that this is the trend, it is encouraging, since it can be expected to facilitate and enhance the intrinsic value of friendships between men and women. But the fact remains that American men and women have not known how to enjoy and appreciate nonromantic friendships. Some women, especially those who are well-educated, have tried to establish this kind of friendship, but usually the response has been either sexual and love proposals or a total lack of interest. Because they valued the interaction with the men involved, some reluctantly accepted a sexual and affective relationship (Seidenberg, 1972; Safilios-Rothschild, 1972). However, in some cases in which women have formed a friendship with a man (especially with an attractive man), they have felt insulted and rejected if there was no clear indication that the man was sexually or affectively interested in them (even if he did not behaviorally express those interests owing to a variety of social constraints). Thus, while women have been relatively more interested in and appreciative of other-sex friendships than men, they have also tended to be ambivalent and dissatisfied when these friendships were totally devoid of underlying or potential sexual and love elements.

Here it must be noted that the reasons for which men have not typically sought or especially valued friendships with women are not limited to their masculine sex-role stereotypes and socialization experiences. Women have not particularly valued other women's friendship either because of the prevailing notion that women are of less value than men. Thus, men were the "desirable" friends for both men and women and women felt quite proud of a male friend.

In traditional societies in which women have been and are almost entirely excluded from the world of men (except as sexual objects or servants), they have learned to value and depend upon close relationships with other women. But whenever it is possible to have men as friends, women have clearly preferred them over women. Their motivations have been complex. Men have always been desirable as friends because such friendships were often viewed as a prelude to or potential for future love relationships. In fact, many women report that long and close friendships between men and women that eventually develop into romantic love relationships tend to be strong and good. In a way, friendships with men were some sort of insurance for the future, in case actual love or marital relationships did not work out satisfactorily or were disrupted. Also, women enjoy friendships with men because such relationships sometimes represent their acceptance by men as an equal and a worthwhile partner and companion without the contaminating influence of expressed sexuality. Any underlying sexual overtones reassure women, on the other hand, of their attractiveness for men other than their husband and/or lover.

The existence of sexual and affective overtones need not interfere with the establishment and enjoyment of friendships between men and women. As a matter of fact, they may be necessary for some friendships; or they may add considerably to the dimensions and enjoyment of the relationship (Pankin, 1973). However, what *can* interfere are the expectations the friends, as well as the people around them, hold concerning the realization of sexual and love interests. When men and women can handle the existence of these overtones and when those around them can accept such friendships at face value, it is possible to relax and appreciate the relationship, even with the occasional sexual and/or romantic overtones.

When people believe, as a result of their upbringing and the prevailing sex-role stereotypes, that "something is wrong" unless a sexual or a love relationship develops between a man and woman who are in a nonromantic friendship, the situation will be strained and difficult. In fact, the two involved may grow to see the friendship as a "stalemate" or a failure, and cease eventually to appreciate what it offers. To avoid this, as we have mentioned above, friends must resist the pressures of those around them to gravitate toward a sexual relationship, if they are both unmarried (Bell, 1975). If friends are already married to other people, then the pressures on them to dissolve their friendship are enormous. Marital partners, relatives, and acquaintances find it hard to accept the existence of such friendships. Spouses particularly resent them because of the existing close ties and the sharing of experiences, even when they are convinced that there are no sexual or love elements. They typically feel that another person is taking over an important part of the intimate relationship with "their" mate. Furthermore, men and women friends (especially if they are not married to other people) usually spend a lot of time together and share many experiences that are usually shared by lovers. This becomes an additional factor that conditions them and pushes them toward a romantic relationship or the breakup of the friendship (Paine, 1969).

Other types of complications that threaten the survival of a friendship between a man and a woman emerge when only one of them wants and attempts to transform the friendship into a sexual or love relationship but the other is reluctant to do so. In these cases, only rarely does the friendship survive because the one who proposes the changes may feel rejected. This is particularly true for men, whose idea of masculinity does not allow them to accept that a woman's lifelong friendship may be as (or more) valuable than a short-lived sexual or love relationship. Too many friendships have been wasted in this way—rich and meaningful relationships that would have provided wonderful experiences for the people involved.

A fundamental difficulty in the establishment and survival of friendships between men and women is the monolithic love model by which we have been taught to abide. The Western version of the love model requires not only sexual and affective exclusivity but also companionship exclusivity, so that there is little room even for close, intimate friends. As we have already mentioned, this tendency has sometimes been carried so far in the United States that very close friendships even with members of the same sex have been considered undesirable and suspect. American couples are expected to *be* best friends; they usually have other friends whom they see socially, but even when any of these become close, the couple shares them so that one spouse does not feel left out. Exclusive friends aren't allowed.

In view of all the structural and psychological obstacles that interfere with the establishment and survival of nonromantic friendships between men and women, it seems almost a miracle when they succeed. Up to now, there have been some special situations that tended to facilitate such friendships. Men and women sometimes found it easier to become good friends after they had stopped being lovers or spouses. The earlier sexual or love relationship can help reduce or minimize the sexual tension between them and leave them free and relaxed to enjoy a relationship without hangups and inhibitions. As a matter of fact, in some cases, previously mismatched lovers and spouses have been known to form healthy friendships once the sexual and love elements were removed. Another special situation has been the ease some men found in having nonsexual relationships with older women. Such friendships were not only socially approved but even encouraged, and enriched the lives of both people. Today, however, in our present transitional stage, the sexuality of older women is increasingly recognized, so with the introduction of sexual possibilities such friendships may experience considerable strain. There are indications that older women, especially if they are vital and interesting, are increasingly viewed as attractive and desirable.

Probably, as many more men and women come to enjoy an equal social status, we can expect that many more will want to develop friendships with the other sex. Only when such friendships have become a perfectly acceptable and highly valued form of interaction between men and women will sexual and love relationships truly become options. As long as male-female friendships are strenuous, difficult, and at best ambiguous, men and women who are attracted to each other for a variety of reasons will be pressured and obliged to opt for sex and/or love when many might have preferred a fulfilling friendship (Safilios-Rothschild, 1972).

Six

THE PERILS
OF TRANSITION

New Questions and New Answers

The different types of social changes taking place every day in the roles of men and women, the nature of marriage and the family, attitudes toward parenthood, and human sexuality raise a great number of new questions for which there are not always answers. Because many of these changes are only emerging and are by no means crystallized yet, people are still struggling to understand their meaning and are experimenting with answers. Men and women are faced daily with new situations and are forced to cope with changes and options for which they are not psychologically prepared.

The fact that many alternatives have not yet been tried out, much less fully accepted and institutionalized, is for many people threatening and anxiety-provoking. For those who have been socialized to believe that only one answer or one option can be right and acceptable, the present tendency toward a multiplicity of options is deemed disorienting and even destructive. The younger generation feels more at ease with having a choice from among many possibilities and with moving from one possibility to another. Perhaps this generation will be more comfortable and better able to prepare the next to cope and to make different decisions at different stages of their lives.

Young people's efforts to experience love, intimacy, and meaning in their sexual relationships are complicated by their prevailing negative reactions to the togetherness, possessiveness, and mutual subjugation and oppression that have traditionally characterized love and marriage relationships. The ideal is to love but be "cool" and never allow oneself to drown in passion, possessiveness, or jealousy or become dependent upon the loved one.

Bengis (1972) believes that young people want to be free and committed at the same time. They do not want to imprison themselves or the one they love in a love relationship; they want it to exist out of choice and as an expression of freedom. They want to stay faithful, and to express concern, affection, and a sense of responsibility as a free expression of love rather than because the other demands it or makes it a condition for the very existence of the relationship. Finally, young people admire lovers who can "split" without recriminations and scenes when their relationship is not working out anymore.

A beautiful, ideal conception of love, some would say; a cold, inhuman conception others (probably older persons) might aver. But whatever the evaluation, it is a difficult type of love relationship to establish and, even more so, to maintain. For teenagers to young adults in their 20s and early 30s, this new love model is stressful, frustrating, and often painful. Many young people are finding that it is not so easy to separate love from possessiveness; from the need to be together with the one they love (even where the other needs freedom to explore); from the need to be continuously reassured that they are loved; or from emotional dependence on the loved one. And they have trouble being cool about sex when they love; they need the physical intimacy, the touching, the sexual loving. They hurt when the other tells them about a minor, insignificant infidelity or a casual sexual encounter, despite all their intellectual acceptance of "freedom." And they go to pieces when the one they love wants to leave or when they both see that the relationship is disintegrating or is becoming destructive.

Such open, honest, free, and undemanding love relationships are difficult to achieve and maintain, possibly because we do not know yet how to handle them. The lack of institutional and legal props, as well as of conventional expectations and rules, leave us naked and alone in front of the ones we love. Thus many people are fearful of loving, of failing, of the intense feeling, suffering, and separation a love relationship may bring (Bengis, 1972). Some "cop out" by marrying and establishing more or less conventional involvements and occasionally achieving a comfortable, viable relationship by means of a series of continuous compromises. Others, especially many of the young women who are struggling with their own liberation, resent becoming emotionally dependent upon the one they love as "unliberated" women have always done. They are afraid of becoming weak and vulnerable in love, because they may be manipulated and exploited. They are afraid because most men are still not rid of their masculine "hangups," and love relationships are not yet free of dominance and power preoccupations. As a result, during the transition that we are undergoing, many men and women are afraid to love. These fears are accentuated in women who, once in love, may want to please the man and suppress their individuality and ambitions, but they hesitate because this means lack of independence and a too-heavy involvement that binds and may not be enjoyable. And because the more they give and the more they sacrifice, the more they tend to expect of the other. Despite all their efforts to stay "cool," many find that, once in love, they gravitate toward the old emotional exclusivity with all its trappings — jealousy, possessiveness, demands, and dependence. Some have found that the only way to stay "cool" with the one they love is to have simultaneous sexual or sexual-affective relationships with several other men who usually remain marginal to the main relationship. Some women manage this game quite well; others do not, and the emotional confusion overpowers them because they do not have the necessary skills to handle this level of emotional complexity (Bengis, 1972).

A considerable number of American women in their 30s, 40s, and even 50s are experiencing the problems that go along with the current social changes. Many are trying to redefine their lives in terms of new insights about themselves in a world in which they have traditionally been second-class citizens. Some of them, after ten or fifteen or more years of traditional marriage, have tried to renegotiate their marriage contracts so that the loving-sexual relationship with their husbands would not interfere but instead facilitate their development and self- actualization. Many have failed. Those who have succeeded attribute their success to the fact that their husbands loved them very much and were willing to undergo possibly painful psychological changes that led to a redefinition of the relationship. Some lucky few had husbands who were flexible and who lacked the traditional sexist psychological resistances and thus found it easier to accept the changed division of labor and responsibilities resulting from the negotiation. These rare men were able to see and appreciate the new balance of psychological, social, and economic advantages and costs.*

Many of those women who have failed in their efforts to change the marital structure and relationship have opted for divorce. This too has led to a new set of challenges — involving such things as finding a job, facing too much independence and loneliness, and coping with the dating business all over again. At this point many women — particularly those who are unwilling to

---

*It is striking to note that no research is available regarding the socialization experiences, the personalities, and situational contexts conducive to men's ability to redefine their marital roles as well as their relationship with their wives.

play the indifference and hard-to-get courtship games at which they may have excelled at an earlier age — become disillusioned and frustrated with their sexual and love relationships. They find that an open and honest expression of love and pleasure may get them nowhere; and occasionally they are even rejected for other women who still play the old femininity games. Some come to the bitter and painful conclusion that in the present phase of social transition, the only rewarding, secure, and satisfactory relationships are friendships. Only friends can remain honest, open, and caring and appreciative of an open, free exchange of thoughts and feelings. Some women are able to establish such rich and rewarding friendships only with women, others form them with both men and women. And many deliberately keep their sexual relationships devoid of affective elements because they do not want to complicate and possibly spoil the physical pleasure to be had.

The 1970 census statistics showed that women with five or more years of college education are divorcing more often and remarrying less often than other divorced men and women (U.S. Department of Commerce, 1972; Glick, 1975). The high divorce rates and low remarriage rates of highly educated women are especially obvious in the 35 to 44 age group (Glick, 1975). Their abstinence from a second marriage is partly due to structural and partly to social and psychological factors. The structural factor is the relatively limited number of available men with an equal or higher education and at the same age or older who are willing to marry women in their late 30s or early 40s instead of much younger women — sex objects. The social and psychological factors include women's disillusionment with marriage and mate expectations and behaviors; complications and impediments to their careers resulting from trying to be a wife and mother as well as a successful professional person; and a reluctance to give up their new-found freedom and autonomy, to renegotiate their lifestyle and to have to make a number of significant compromises (Marciano, 1975). Their not remarrying is, therefore, partly out of choice and partly out of dissatisfaction with existing options. Some of those highly educated women are choosing one of the following "new" options: (1) a homosexual relationship; or (2) a love relationship with a much younger man, such as a graduate student or a young professional man starting on his career. Both options go against many powerful taboos; the latter represents an ingenious solution that copes with many structural problems and helps broaden the base of "eligible" men. Despite the fact that these younger men usually have a lower status than the women, this discrepancy does not create difficulties, probably in part because the younger men have (at least theoretically) the potential of eventually reaching a higher status than the women and in part because in their new maturity and freedom of choice of mates, some women are able to give less importance to traditional standards of social and economic "success."

It is hoped that this phenomenon of educated women not choosing to remarry is the result of the current transitional strains rather than a symptom of a serious and profound malaise between educated men and women. Increasingly, professional women may have a wider pool of men (including young men and liberated men) from among whom they can choose a second partner so that their decision whether or not to remarry represents a clear choice.

Women in general tend to be relatively somewhat better prepared psychologically for the ongoing changes because of the ideology of the women's movement. They have a certain degree of awareness brought about by means of endless discussions and writing revolving around their changing roles. Men, on the other hand, are not prepared as well to face the tremendous problems of this transition period—partly because of their socialization experiences, which inhibit them from being introspective and from being able to discuss their feelings, emotions, fears, and weaknesses. Also, there is only a very small "men's liberation movement" that reaches very few men. Men are at present caught between two worlds. Many are, in fact, being yanked forcibly out of the old world by women. They are propelled into a "new order" that is not always well defined or well understood.

Many men in their 30s, 40s, and 50s are first faced with new questions and puzzles when their wives start being restless or downright unhappy with the marital routine and begin to explore the possibility of changing the rules and redefining the relationship. At that point, many husbands—often for the first time—have to ask fundamental questions about the nature of their relationship to women, their own sexuality, the extent to which they are loved and can love, as well as about love and sexuality in general. Some men are able to come to understand the woman's point of view. They are able to redefine their own and their wives' roles as well as their relationship, and to enjoy the new advantages and opportunities gained by the change without being afraid of the costs attached to these changes. These men emerge freer and more confident of themselves and the relationship with their wives.

Quite a few husbands, however, are not able to change their ideas about the roles of men and women and the marriage relationship Their socialization has certainly not prepared them to function except within the context of the traditional masculine role, and they may not be able to cope with anything that threatens this role. The basis for the marriage has been so thoroughly grounded in the traditional ideal of woman as a sex object and a servant that the moment she is no longer willing to play these roles the marriage falls to pieces. Sometimes the whole process has come up too suddenly and its course has run too quickly for them to catch up with it, to understand it and accept it. Those husbands who resist redefining their marital relationship so as to allow a rearrangement of rights and responsibilities that will allow their wives (and sometimes also themselves) more space and growth and independence, may well face the pain of being rejected and divorced by their wives. Then they must try to understand what went wrong, what happened and why. This is especially true for those men who still love their wives, who have had what they thought was a good love and sex relationship. Many never achieve an understanding of how or why a woman would want "to be herself." Furthermore, their inability to understand what is going on is compounded by the fact that their ex-wives have chosen to struggle for a living that often is at a much lower standard than the one they had enjoyed throughout marriage.

Most often these experiences pretty badly shake the men who undergo them, since suddenly everything they ever learned or took for granted is negated. It is hard for them to comprehend why loving a woman, being a good lover, and providing adequately for her may not be enough to make her happy or to keep her. They do not know what it is women want. A common way of coping with a wife's quest for autonomy, independence, exploration of potential, and deep need for development is to interpret it as a subterfuge for an actual or desired sexual and love relationship with another man. Their masculine pride does not allow them to believe that a woman they loved could abandon emotional, economic, and sexual security for something so elusive as autonomy and self-actualization (Goldberg, 1976).

Most divorced men usually remarry on the average within two years, and well-educated men remarry more often than other men (Norton and Glick, 1976). What kind of women do they marry the second time around, and what types of relationships are they able to establish? Some men, profoundly disturbed by the reasons behind their divorce, manage by themselves or with some psychiatric help to understand the meaning of the divorce as well as the meaning of the changing roles of men and women. Some not only come to understand "what women want" but also to accept and like the ensuing new roles and relationships and to grow as human beings. Such men then are able to seek women who will help them further integrate these new insights into experiences. Then they are often able to establish a totally new type of love and marriage relationship.

Most men, however, feel no special pressure to understand and change—they can fairly easily find attractive and desirable women who are willing to have sexual and/or love relationships with them on *their* conditions—the old way. Sufficient number of attractive women are still willing to re-create the traditional kind of love-sex relationship. We can hypothesize that most probably these women are not highly educated and have no career aspirations or they would pose the same conditions and make the same demands as the former wives at the breaking point. Or they may be younger women who have not experienced the stresses and frustrations of a traditional relationship. As long as attractive, desirable women are willing to become traditional wives, many men will not be motivated to change.

Having discussed some of the major trends and current resulting strains in love relationships, especially within marriage, we can now look at the phases through which male and female sexuality is going, and the potential — both constructive and destructive — this transitional period has for love relationships.

The Performance Trap:
Women Must Also Perform

Traditionally in most societies a woman has had to be satisfied with whatever kind of sexual performance the man was capable of and could not complain about or criticize his performance. This was because women had been conceptualized as having very few, if any, sexual drives, needs, and appetites.* In the Victorian era, it was commonly thought that women had no sex drive; they were taught to tolerate men's sexual needs as part of marital duty.

Furthermore, the standards of sexual activity have been vastly disparate. Women of the past were supposed to have had *no* sexual contact with men. Therefore, when they were married, they were supposed to be initiated into sex by the husband and to

---

*In West Africa, however, women have been considered to have the stronger and more intense sexual drives and needs. Therefore, when they were widowed or divorced, they were allowed and even expected to have lovers. This behavior was considered natural and necessary not only to satisfy their sexual drives but also so they could choose a new marital partner.

be satisfied with whatever his sexual ability and performance happened to be. Since they had no standards and previous experience by which to judge his performance, it was in fact much easier for them to feel "satisfied" because they "didn't know any better."

Women were not socialized to expect men to please them—instead, their "feminine" training had conditioned them to try hard to please men even by pretending about everything, including their own pleasure and orgasms. They were not geared to expect great sexual satisfaction and when sexual relationships left them totally indifferent, frustrated, or even disgusted, they tended to assume it was their fault. Because so many of their female friends shared their fate, they often assumed that it was "normal" to be sexually unsatisfied, if indeed they ever considered their own satisfaction or pleasure as a possibility. Sex was for men, and women had to bear it because they needed men. Even those rare women who felt sexually frustrated and perceived that there might be specific reasons for this—such as, for example, the man's lack of concern with foreplay and the woman's readiness for intercourse, or the man's fast ejaculation—did not dare to criticize the man, especially with regard to his sexual performance. The stronger the sex-role stereotypes, the more men tend to define themselves in terms of genital sexuality and sexual performance and the more violently they have tended to react to any negative comment concerning their sexual role.

According to traditional sex-role stereotypes, "good" women were not expected to play an active sexual role, to have any special sexual skills and competencies, or even to enjoy too intensely. Display of such characteristics and behaviors would automatically earn them the undesirable label of "badness." Stereotypically feminine women were not, therefore, expected to "perform" sexually, except to simulate (modest) pleasure at appropriate moments. Furthermore, women have been expected in middle age to relinquish their claims to sexuality. While the prevailing sex-role stereotypes allowed men to enjoy sex for as long as they wanted, women after (or even before) menopause were supposed to become completely asexual beings. Since in traditional societies married women have had (and still do in many Third-World nations) a child or a pregnancy every year, by the time they reached 40 it was small wonder that this release from sexual responsibility was considered a great relief—they were worn out! The achievement of this "asexual" status for women has often granted them a relatively greater freedom of speech and of movement, as well as access to some family and economic power especially in traditional societies in which the status of women is generally low (Bart, 1969; Safilios-Rothschild, 1977). This improvement in their position made this "asexual" label attractive enough for women to be willing to suppress their undiminished sexuality.

However, women have become increasingly aware of their sexuality. The changing sex roles allow women a greater latitude of sexual expression. As women are no longer obsessed with the fear of pregnancy, they enjoy their sexuality and express it in a variety of experiences. They are discovering that they can function very differently and experience varying amounts of pleasure in different types of sexual relationships. Studies of "swinging" couples (Bartell, 1971) have shown that when women are in a situation in which they are allowed and even encouraged by their husbands to be sexually active with a number of different men, they do so and are able to experience a tremendous amount of sexual pleasure. While at the beginning women hesitate to "swing" and must often be pushed by their husbands, once in the permissive context they enjoy it even more than their husbands and want to continue it even after their husbands would prefer to stop. They are able to unfold sexually by discovering and realizing their sexual potential with different partners with whom they are not emotionally involved. This enjoyment of sex for its own sake to the exclusion of other considerations, is a novelty for women who have had to justify sex in terms of love or economic and social security in marriage. But while information from studies on swinging is quite informative about female sexuality, swinging affects the lives of only a small percentage of women. Many more have learned a great deal from Masters' and Johnson's findings concerning the greater orgasmic capacity of women and the continuation of sexual desires, needs, and ability in women throughout life. Such public acknowledgement of female sexuality allows women to admit their sexual feelings and needs and to expect an active sexual life up to and throughout middle age and after. However, the new freedom is not without its problems. In their new-found eagerness to discover and enjoy their sexuality during the current social transition, women occasionally tend to overemphasize sexual performance and pleasure. They sometimes set expectations that are too high. For example, many feel that multiple orgasms are a necessary part of a sexual encounter; failing to achieve this goal, which they may consider their right, many blame the men involved. In other words, they are accepting equal right to sexual expression and pleasure but not equal active sexual responsibility. Thus performance becomes the sole male responsibility and men are judged on the basis of definite and high standards. This makes for unrealistic standards of sexual behavior, strain, and unhappiness and it becomes a major threat to men.

At present, this increasing openly admitted desire for sexual activity and pleasure on the part of women in midlife is usually badly timed in that it takes place at exactly the point when men are experiencing some physiological changes in their sexual ability. They are caught at a time when they have to face self-doubts and a diminished confidence in sexual performance. The resulting anxiety often becomes a panic leading to impotence or coping behavior such as liaisons with much younger and more sexually inexperienced women who may not make many sexual demands on them and, therefore, do not threaten them (Sheehy, 1976). As long as women cannot accept the responsibilities of sexuality in terms of active sexual performance, many men (except possibly the very young) may be unable to cope with the resulting unrealistic sexual demands and expectations. Strains will abound and seriously interfere with men's and women's ability to enjoy sex and to successfully integrate it into love relationships.

During the transition women's preoccupation with sexual satisfaction may in some cases interfere with their ability to establish loving relationships with genuine commitment. Some women may choose at least some men as sex objects, but be unwilling to make social and emotional commitments to them. In fact these women separate sexuality from love or from companionship. In this way, some women now choose to separate sexuality from love for very different reasons than in the traditional past. This separation provides them with more flexibility and a variety of relationships. Also, some women turn to other women for sexual satisfaction. Sometimes this is expressed as a brief experience and occasionally it becomes a more stable and meaningful exclusive or alternate love relationship (Bartell, 1973; Blumstein and Schwartz, 1976).

Another important emerging change is that as the sexual double standard breaks down and women feel increasingly free to express their sexuality and to experience sexual satisfaction, women are no longer exempt from "performance" requirements. While traditionally women's sexual ignorance and ineptitude often enhanced their attractiveness and desirability, the same traits, except in very young women, are considered unacceptable today. Women have started feeling the pressure to be sexually experienced, skilled, and competent. Already in the American culture, virginity after age 20 is viewed with increasing ambivalence; some even consider it an indication of undesirability and incompetence (Laws, 1970). Books, manuals, and sex therapists are trying to teach women how to perform better and how to actively enhance the male sexual performance. Women are in this way starting to share the performance anxieties that men have always experienced (Laws, 1970). Women are also admonished by "Total Woman" type literature as well as by "how-to" sex books to play an active sexual role (Maynard, 1975), but not all women are psychologically able to accept this change entirely and many are ambivalent about what their sexual role ought to be. A recent *Redbook* survey of 100,000 mostly middle-class American women indicated, for example, that the overwhelming majority (about 90 percent) of them take the initiative and play an active role during sexual intercourse (R. Bell, 1975). But another recent study of a small but "representative" sample of Berkeley women college students showed that over 40 percent disapproved or did not feel comfortable about "getting the sexual ball rolling" and did not feel "they could let their partner know exactly what turned them on" (*"Female Pleasure Patterns,"* 1975). Many women still feel uncomfortable when they play an active sexual role; they are concerned about appearing to be oversexed, demanding, and may fear threatening the man. And men are equally ambivalent in their reactions toward sexually active and skilled women.

In general, the expectation that women are equally responsible for the quality of sexual performance is healthy. During the present transition, however, there is the danger that sex will become a test situation in which both must display their skills and try to excel in performance instead of relaxing and letting feelings and emotions permeate, guide, and enrich the sexual experience. If this competitive achievement orientation can be overcome, men and women may be able to share the responsibility of sexual performance and reach a greater degree of intimacy and pleasure through understanding.

The New Threats to Men

The prevailing sexual double standard and sex-role stereotypes have traditionally inhibited women from evaluating men's sexual performance, as we mentioned earlier. Women were not supposed to have had the necessary sexual experience that would enable them to evaluate quality—and even if they did, they could not admit it. Until very recently, women have found more socially acceptable reasons for breaking up relationships when in fact the only reason was their sexual dissatisfaction.

Today, however, women increasingly feel free to admit (or

boast of) their sexual experiences with different men. Some may exaggerate their sexual experience and skills and may misuse them by transforming them into a dangerous psychological weapon. Under the guise of "liberation," some women take a special, perverse pleasure in comparing the sexual ability of a present lover to that of previous lovers and to taunt him with his shortcomings. It is one thing to communicate the existence of sexual problems and pleasures; but it is a different matter to use the new openness to make another person feel inadequate, guilty, or competitive. Women, of course, in this way defend themselves against the usual accusation of "frigidity" thrown at them whenever anything goes wrong with the sexual interaction. By asserting their previous satisfactory sexual relations with other men, women are no longer vulnerable to accusations of frigidity and cannot take the blame for unsatisfactory sexual experiences.

The price paid for such dangerous sexual games is often quite high. For many men, who may base their masculinity on sexual performance, it can be disastrous. This is a new weapon for those women who may in the past have used standards of money and success as comparison points. Men were deeply hurt by these comparisons when they were rated low. But apparently unfavorable comparison in terms of sexual performance can hurt even more, since in this case it is more difficult for the man to blame society, his boss, the state of the economy, or the government for his failure. A recent study of American college students showed that men often tend to compare, with considerable anxiety, their sexual performance with the imaginary sexual performance of their girlfriends' ex-lovers even when their girlfriends do not make such explicit comparisons. Because of the anxiety this generates, some young men openly admit that they prefer sexually inexperienced young women who do not threaten them with past sexual exploits (Komarovsky, 1976). This admission of men's preference for sexually inexperienced women sheds a new light on the traditional desirability of virginity. Sometimes the reaction to implicit or explicit sexual comparison is impotence. And the existence of impotence is further complicated because its cause may be anxiety produced by stressful sexual demands and/or a subconscious desire to punish the woman who is making the demands. In this way impotence becomes a mechanism of social control. Men seem to say by their impotence that unless women are willing to go back to their sexually passive and subordinate position, they are going to be punished by being altogether deprived of sexual experience and satisfaction (Lipman-Blumen, 1976). In any case, the threat and anxiety produced in men by destructive sexual comparisons are harmful to both partners as well as to the relationship itself.

During the last few years, physicians, psychiatrists, and family counselors have been reporting increased impotence; this is usually blamed on the women's movement, and the increased demands for high level of sexual performance (Ginsberg et al., 1972). While this explanation may be true, it is also oversimplified. The nature of the social and psychological dynamics involved is much more complex. Both men and women have to cope with drastic shifts in sexual standards and behavioral patterns for which they are not psychologically prepared. Women may sometimes overreact to their newly discovered and expressed sexual needs and desires and to the depth of their sexual potential. And most men have not been able yet to bring about the necessary changes in their behaviors, standards and expectations that could allow them to feel comfortable and to enjoy women's affirmation of their sexuality. In this way, instead of leading to greater sexual enjoyment for both men and women, these ongoing changes often lead to paralyzing fears and sexual dysfunctioning.

Men become anxious about their sexual functioning when they can no longer determine when they will have sexual relations as well as the intensity, duration, and type of sexual relations. Even young men do not seem to be exempt from such fears. A recent study of American college students showed that young men in 1970 were still emotionally repelled and threatened by women's sexual initiative (Komarovsky, 1976). The loss of exclusive control over sexual encounters represents a new and powerful threat to men because they may be asked to have sex when they do not feel like it or are not up to it. Many men have not learned how to say no to a woman's sexual proposition because they are still "hung up" on the masculine all- powerful sexual image. Having to refuse sex becomes such a threatening possibility that impotence becomes a less painful way out of an impossible situation.

It is to be hoped that many of the present transitional strains and difficulties will be overcome and that the redefinition of values, roles, and relationships will create more options and alternatives and facilitate the road toward better relationships between men and women.

Seven

THE FUTURE
FOR LOVE AND SEX

We have seen that there are important changes going on in men-women relationships. More and more, the traditional sex-role stereotypes, as well as the famous "double standard," are losing their strongholds. The results of this dual change are far-reaching and are leading to the restructuring of men's and women's behaviors, as well as to drastic redefinitions of the relationships between them. As the notions of masculinity and femininity become increasingly meaningless, men's and women's behaviors are converging and covering the same range. The potential changes in love and sexual expression are only now emerging, and the ongoing transitions are still incomplete. During the present phase of the transition, we find that there is no longer one monolithic model of love and/or sexuality; many different models are evolving, some of which may be only transitory and experimental and may never become generally accepted, viable alternatives. As we discussed in the last chapter, the trend today is toward the availability and acceptance of several options. Yet psychologists, sociologists, psychiatrists, sex therapists, and philosophers continue to try to specify a single "ideal" model of love and commitment as the most valid (Francoeur and Francoeur, 1974; Kilpatrick, 1975; Masters and Johnson, 1975). Probably the availability of alternative and equally acceptable models of love and sexual relationships is baffling to most people, including social scientists and therapists. Our socialization has not prepared us to cope with many options. We are conditioned to search for the one we think best, and we are not content unless we have convinced everybody else that *our* model is best for everyone!

Sex for the Sake of Sex

Despite the overall unclear picture, there are some general trends that allow us to delineate the nature of emerging and future intimate, loving, and sexual relationships. Probably the most fundamental change to take place will be a freeing of sexuality of its instrumentality, for both men and women. Women in a nonsexist society will no longer rely upon their sexuality in order to get "a piece of the pie." The decreasing importance attached to virginity and the decline of the sexual double standard will allow women to have sexual relationships that are not necessarily associated with or leading toward marriage (Fox, 1975). Sexuality will no longer be the primary resource to be used in the negotiations toward commitment and marriage, but rather an expression of emotions to be enjoyed. Most men in a nonsexist society will stop associating sex with power; because women will be freer to choose, men will have far less opportunity to use sex to dominate. Sexual relations will thus no longer be characterized by the dominant/submissive relationship between men and women that exists today.

We should state at this point that there will probably always be men and women who still· use sex to get economic security, status, or power. And we are not implying that sexual relationships will become devoid of social and psychological commitments and responsibilities. Such commitments and responsibilities may be undertaken by men *and* women. Since in a nonsexist society women as a class will not necessarily become socially, psychologically, and financially dependent upon men, even after bearing children, other criteria than gender will determine the nature of responsibility and the person(s) who will shoulder it. We can expect that women will be increasingly socialized not only to take the psychological risk of initiating sexual and love relationships but also to undertake the ensuing responsibilities. And men will be socialized to be prepared for responsibility and commitment toward human beings of an equal status; presumably many will even consider the option of themselves becoming socially, psychologically, and/or financially dependent upon a woman. At the present stage in the transition we see an increasing trend toward the right to equal sexual satisfaction and self-determination; in the future an optimistic forecast would include a greater reciprocity in the assumption of the responsibilities as well as in the enjoyment of rights.

Perhaps the most important aspect of the changing men-women relationship is the fact that the commitments and responsibilities we have been talking about should spontaneously ensue from the new type of relationship that is evolving between men and women rather than from the sheer fact that they have had sexual intercourse or from legal or social constraints.* Eventually men and women will learn to share the advantages as well as the "costs" of a relationship. Once sex is no longer a major commodity, people will be able to enjoy it for its own sake; it will represent the free exchange of self-expression, a giving and receiving, a joyous experience rather than an arena for the old manipulative power games.

Having set the basic principle of the emerging mode of sexual expression, we can now examine in more detail the charac-

---

*There are indications that this has already been achieved to some extent in Sweden (See Chapter 4).

teristics of the intimate, loving, and sexual relationships between men and women that can emerge out of our present transitional period.

Women Can Also Pursue

As we saw in Chapter 6, it has become increasingly accept-able for women to initiate sexual relations within the confines of a marital relationship. Within the context of nonmarital rela-tionships, however, many women still do not dare openly admit their sexual desires and preferences — and do not let themselves experience many orgasms unless they are seriously committed to the relationship — because of a fear of being viewed as "over-sexed" and mistrusted as long-term companions (*Female Pleasure Patterns,* 1975). The trend is clearly, however, for women to feel increasingly more comfortable about expressing their sexuality and preferences by assuming an active sexual role, as well as by initiating sexual relations within the context of all kinds of relationships (R. Bell, 1975).

But when it comes to pursuing men, women still have a long way to go before they can feel comfortable to do so and to leave themselves open to the hurt of rejection. A woman's discomfort in pursuing a man to whom she is attracted may be surpassed on-ly by the pursued man's discomfort and fear. Most men are still unable to relax, enjoy, and be flattered by an attractive woman's pursuit. It all too often represents a threat — probably because it tends to diminish the extent of the man's control (or the extent to which he thinks he has control) over the choice of the woman he loves, makes love to, or marries. Of course, men can accept or re-ject a woman's proposal. But most have not yet learned how to first carefully evaluate a woman's proposition and then, if they find it unattractive, to gracefully refuse. Their tendency has been to run away and to devalue the woman in order to justify their irrational fear and flight. The devaluation usually follows this theme: If the woman pursues me (or any man), it must mean that something is wrong with her and she has to do this because no man is interested in her. This may be a carry-over from the traditional past, when only "bad" women were sexually aggressive and could "go after" men and good, wholesome women never did. As long as the pursuing women were clearly "bad," the attracted men often had a sexual relationship with them, usually of short duration. But at present when the label of "badness" has become both ambiguous and meaningless, men usually cope in two ways with the threat posed by pursuing attractive women. One is to neutralize them by devaluing them as "undesirable rejects" in the love-sex market. And the other is to treat them as the "bad" women of the past by having a sexual but *not* a love relationship with them. Within the confines of such a limited relationship, men can feel relatively at ease since sexuality has always been considered a "masculine" domain within which they can move comfortably and freely. The limitation of the relationship to a purely sexual one and the control over any possible emotions also imply that the relationship is not a "serious" one destined to last long. In this way, the woman involved and her threatening, aggressive behavior tend to be minimized in importance and meaning, and, hence, to become more or less neutralized.

A man's inability to enjoy being pursued by a woman as much as pursuing one is most often coupled with his inability to occasionally play an exclusively or partially passive sexual role and "let things happen to him." For a man to be able to play and enjoy a sexually passive role, he must be able to give up his desire to dominate the situation and the woman and open himself up to receiving and experiencing. Most men still have troubles relinquishing control in sexual encounters. When they believe they have lost the lead, they are apt to also lose the ability to surrender themselves and enjoy the sexual experience. Deeply ingrained sex-role stereotypes make men feel threatened and vulnerable when they are no longer the dominant, powerful person in a sexual interaction and these feelings interfere with spontaneity and pleasure. Sometimes men react with impotence to a woman's playing an active sexual role or taking the top position in intercourse (Bach and Goldberg, 1975). In this way they attempt to recapture the dominant, controlling position in the sexual relationship. On the other side of the coin, many women are not comfortable in playing an active sexual role—probably because their lingering sex-role socialization may make them feel in a way cheated, less desired, and less loved. Women's socialization as sex objects still lingers, and some women still find it difficult to be "turned on" sexually unless a man *makes love to them.* Their transition from sex objects to sex subjects is slow and difficult. Dominance and submission have been too deeply ingrained in sexual relations, and we have only recently started sorting out the dynamics involved.

What is the forecast? The gradual breakdown of sex-role stereotypes should make for an increasingly greater role flexibility that would facilitate interchangeability between passive and active roles in initiating relationships as well as in playing out specific roles. As masculinity and femininity become meaningless concepts, men and women should feel free to pursue and be pursued; to choose and be chosen; to alternate between active and passive sexual roles; and to take the risk of being rejected while at other times having to refuse and reject. Rejecting a love and/or sexual proposal or being rejected will no longer imply frigidity or sexual inadequacy or less "masculinity" or "femininity," but will simply be the exercise of an option. As these patterns become institutionalized, the gloomy forecasts of some social scientists— namely, that when women aggressively pursue men, men will tend to become coy and hesitant, or simply satiated and bored with the totally available "commodity" of sex (Rosenfeld, 1969)—will be proven wrong. After all, where is it written that all men have to be sexually aggressive or great lovers? Perhaps in the future it will be possible for people to be less "hung up" on the notion that *everyone* should have super-strong sex drives.

Furthermore, the fact that women will have the option of pursuing men does not mean that they will all consistently take it; neither will men entirely give up the option to pursue women. The availability of the option to pursue as well as to be pursued for both men and women will not necessarily lead to such an extravagance of sexual opportunity that satiation and boredom will be the result. The gloomy projections are clearly unfounded and amusing. Their only value lies in the fact that they strongly underline the existing masculine fears in this area.

As the sex stratification system changes, more women gain high social status and power. This fact has many implications. Experience will have enriched women as persons and status will give them a special power, as well as improved self-confidence and self-image. Such women, particularly during middle age or after, will often become attractive and attracted to younger men, and marriages between such successful women and younger men can be expected to increase in the near future, especially as second marriages for the women (Safilios-Rothschild, 1976). Many of these women can be expected to actively pursue the men they find attractive. Some of the men they pursue, particularly the younger ones, will most often have not only less money but also less status and power, and this power differential may be exploited by some women. It is possible that in a few cases men's fears may be realized. At least a few women (as may be true for a few men in the same situation) may be tempted to misuse their status and power in order to gain or maintain sexual access to desirable men. It is within the realm of possibility that those men may experience an alienation and powerlessness similar to what many women know today. While this is possible, it will be the exception rather than the rule, and it does not justify men's fears about being pursued by women. Actually, it can be claimed that psychological and sexual liberation will not have taken place until sex and love are free of all power games and men and women can propose, accept, or refuse each other's proposals without damage to their masculine or feminine identities, self-esteem, or sense of control and power.

Sex: Beyond Performance

As we have seen, during the present transitional stage there is an overemphasis on sexual performance and the attainment of orgasm. "How-to" books and sex clinics represent money-making enterprises because they attempt to cope with the overwhelming sexual preoccupations and anxieties of men and women as they struggle to disentangle themselves from traditional sexual values, sexual fears, inadequacies, and hangups. Many of these coping mechanisms unfortunately accept and perpetuate a narrow "genital" definition of sexuality, the apex of which is orgasm. It is only recently that the exceptional sex therapist has started to recognize that sex therapy that helps people function adequately in the sex act is treating only symptoms and is not necessarily helping people explore and fulfill their sexual potential. Mann and Caplan, co-directors of the Human Sexuality Program of the University of California Medical Center, have spelled out the need for a reconceptualization of sexuality so as "to include not only genital gratification but also sensuality, the exchange of affection, and other dimensions of emotional expression comprising the sexual self." A broader idea of sexuality implies that one's emotions, as well as the perception and definition of the situation, may be the determining factor for the extent to which one will be sexually stimulated and will experience orgasm(s). Hence, as Mann and Caplan point out, it is the cortex rather than the genitals that constitutes the primary human sex organ (Mann and Caplan, 1975). It is probable that this is the direction in which we are moving, and the elimination of sexism and sex-role stereotypes will help change the inflexible pattern that men and women have had to follow up to now. As we move through the different transitional stages, we can be expected to increasingly recognize that touching, caressing, being physically close, looking and talking affectionately, or even thinking of someone with affection or desire may constitute as important expressions of sexuality as any type and degree of sexual stimulation or as the experiencing of orgasm.

It must be underlined that both men and women, and especially men, must be freed from sex-role stereotypes before they can enjoy sexuality in all its expressions. Masculine stereotypes limit sexual expression to genital sexuality and define masculinity in terms of the frequency and variety of penetrations and orgasms with as many different women as possible. Within such a traditional definition, some men do not feel that touching or caressing or even affectionate talking are necessary; they consider it a masculine right to proceed immediately to sexual intercourse instead of wasting time with "silly, feminine" behaviors.* Because the sexual act itself has allowed traditional men to assert themselves and to subjugate women, the expression of sexuality had to be restricted to this brief behavioral event. Partly in compensation for the brevity of the experience, men had to perform frequently and with many different partners, their sexual behavior following the accumulative, "consumer" model (Israel and Eliasson, 1971). According to this model, the more sexual conquests the better, regardless of the quality of the sexual and love relationship.

This exaggerated emphasis on performance has created considerable anxiety in men about their ability to perform. This anxiety has been successfully alleviated in traditional societies by means of the enforced sexual double standard. And because men have married virgins (or women with very limited sexual experience), wives have not been in a position to evaluate the quality of sexual performance, except in extreme cases. It was only in their sexual contacts with "bad" women that traditional men have had to worry most about the quality of their sexual per-

---

*When women say, "All men want is sex," they refer to the fact that some men are primarily interested in genital sex. Women, on the contrary, have been socialized to enjoy and need nongenital sex as much as genital sex and feel frustrated with men's tendency to restrict the range of sexual expression. In some traditional societies, women's sexual needs and desires could be acceptably expressed *only* in the form of nongenital sex, leading to an even greater gap between men's and women's sexual understanding.

formance and how they compared with other men. "Bad" women had had a variety of sexual relationships; they could evaluate the quality of men's performance and insist on a good sexual performance, since usually they could not aspire to a permanent, social, and legal relationship. A high quality of sexual performance was one of the few tangible advantages of the relationship.

During our transitional period, the so-called sexual "emancipation" of women has, as we have seen, increased the performance requirements for both men and women and has often transformed sexual relations into a competitive game. Increasingly, women demand a high level of performance from men but have to pay a heavy price for this, since they also have to respond and perform according to the rules. Thus, at present the level of anxiety is so high for both men and women concerning the quality and variety of their sexual acrobatics that even when this does not lead to sexual malfunctioning, it can interfere with sexual pleasure and even more with the enjoyment of a loving, affectionate relationship. Many women — probably more than men — are currently setting often rigid rules of performance for men and tend to feel cheated if they do not experience orgasm or when the man is not able to "deliver the goods." Possibly, the more active sexual role played now by women tends to make them feel that they are entitled to a greater degree of sexual stimulation and excitement by a highly performing male partner. We have already discussed the necessity for the "new" woman to be willing to bear an equal responsibility in sexual pleasures received and given.

Clearly, only when men and women become free of sex-role stereotypes will they be able to move across a wide range of sexual behaviors in which they will be able to express and enjoy their sexuality in many different ways. For men to lose the notion that erection, penetration, and orgasm are all-important and to feel and enjoy sensuality and sexual stimulation in all its forms, they must first allow themselves to show tenderness, affection, weakness, and love and not to be afraid to be vulnerable to the woman they love. Because genital sexuality has always been defined as a masculine domain and affection and love a feminine domain, the broadening of human sexuality cannot occur except when the traditional ideas of "masculinity" and "femininity" lose their force. Mann and Caplan (1975) point out that as the preoccupation with and anxiety about genital sexual performance decreases and men and women are able to relax and sexually enjoy all contacts with the other person in intimate relationships, the quality of genital sexual performance can also be expected to improve.

Humanizing Sex and Love

Throughout this book we have examined how the traditional notions of masculinity and femininity have tended to dehumanize love and sexuality. An important element of this dehumanization has been the frequent separation of love from sexuality, as well as the isolation of sexuality as a "special" human expression. Probably the most radical change that can come about in human sexuality is its integration into men's and women's total personality and behavior. Such an integration can lead to the expression of sexuality within the context of all other human expressions and behavior rather than separately. Traditionally, it has been reduced sometimes to a minimal importance and other times blown up out of proportion, depending upon gender, age, and certain social considerations. A healthy integration can take place only when men and women cease relating to each other as to sex objects. Socialization free of sex-role stereotypes and the disappearance of sexism in the society are two basic requirements for the beginning of the humanization of sex and love.

How will men and women behave when they no longer relate to each other as sex objects? For one thing, men will no longer judge, appreciate, and be attracted to women primarily in terms of their sexual attractiveness and physical appearance. Instead, intrinsic qualities and social behaviors will more often take on similar importance. Thus, women may be admired and considered desirable, at least by some men, because they are competent and intelligent or because they are successful financially and/or occupationally (Safilios-Rothschild, 1974). This multiplicity of criteria by which women's attractiveness and desirability will be judged will tend to diminish the present exaggerated emphasis placed upon women's looks, grooming, dress, and age. Thus, women will be considered valuable beyond their decorative value as beautiful objects. This will in turn help to free them from the endless preoccupation with appearance and allow them to use time and energy in a variety of other pursuits.

Within reasonable limits, sexual and affective experience as well as age may well be considered valuable assets in a woman in the future, since they tend to increase her sexual and affective skills as well as her ability to understand others, to make compromises, and to make shared relationships easier and more pleasant. An experienced woman knows how to love and how to give and receive pleasure. In such a liberated context, a virgin, rather than possessing a valuable asset, will have to be helped to overcome her "shortcoming" with patience and know-how.

Men, on the other hand, when they no longer define themselves and are defined by others as well-functioning sex machines, may become free to learn how to love one woman and establish and maintain a mutually satisfactory sexual relationship with her. This sexual redefinition of men that would help put the "sexual" element in its right proportion will help men define themselves and be appreciated by women in terms of their understanding, warmth, sensitivity, and companionship. Men will, therefore, be able to enjoy and value a whole range of close relationships with women. These relationships will include different mixes of sexual love, friendship, mutual pleasure, and growth elements.

Furthermore, the "normalization" of human sexuality would imply that men and women should no longer feel any more vulnerable in sexual relationships than they do in other types of associations. Socialization experiences up to now have conditioned people to believe that the physical nakedness involved in sexual relationships as well as the demonstration of deep physical pleasure creates a special type of interaction which is conducive to baring one's soul and feelings and which, therefore increases one's vulnerability. While it is true that many men and women do not open their hearts and souls to each other unless they have a sexual relationship (usually coupled with an affective relationship), this is so because many people still view sexuality as a unique human interaction involving greater risk taking and shared vulnerability conducive to ultimate trusting. This is an unrealistic, romantic evaluation of sexuality that makes it almost the *only* condition for closeness, and, as such, it is a symptom of the overall poverty in the relationships between men and women. A variety of human interactions in different types of relationships should be equally conducive to closeness and self-disclosure. As long as sex-role stereotypes and social inequalities have prohibited men and women from having close friendships, sexual relationships have been the only type of involvement that has allowed them to occasionally come close to each other. However, once the entire range of relationships is equally opened up to men and women, they will be able to achieve a special closeness within the context of different relationships, thus removing the peculiar awe and discomfort of sexual and affective relationships.

The "Hot" and "Cool" Dilemmas of the Future

Right now it is difficult to tell clearly which problems and dilemmas are transitional and which are with us to stay. Even those who are halfway "liberated" have been brought up to believe in the desirability of all the "good" things as defined by traditional values. Most women still believe that the most wonderful thing on earth is to be passionately in love and be loved in return; to be happily married to the one you love and live together "happily ever after." These beliefs and values still more or less influence all of us and sometimes determine our lives and our ability to enjoy ourselves and be happy. We still measure our experiences largely according to traditional standards and values. So when a passionate love becomes a torture through our own possessiveness and jealousy or when it dies because the other person does not reciprocate to the level of our expectations, we feel lost and unhappy, instead of being able to enjoy the few fulfilling and exciting days, weeks, or months of the relationship. We still believe that a "real" love should be "perfect" and should last forever. When a very good marriage stops being good, those in it feel like failures and often even hang on for quite a while because of the inability to face the facts.* When relationships are broken up, the tendency is often to discredit the entire experience. We are not willing to say that a marriage was great for seven years but then it died because we outgrew it or because it changed with time. We cannot feel grateful and richer for the happy years lived and go on from there. We still have a great difficulty in accepting love and happiness on a short-term basis. In fact, the shorter the duration of a loving and happy relationship, the greater is our tendency to discredit altogether the relationship. And when we know that the relationship is necessarily going to be short-lived, most of us are unable to even enjoy it.

Many people, because of a mixture of responsibility and guilt, cannot divorce or even separate from their mates despite the fact that they perceive their marriage as totally dead. Men have been socialized to believe that they are responsible for their wives no matter what, and this sense of masculine responsibility becomes vividly rekindled by the wife's real or imagined illnesses, problems, inability to cope with life, or threats to commit suicide. And wives have known how to manipulate and capitalize

*Up until very recently, the majority of people have stayed in such marriages out of responsibility toward their spouses (especially husbands), young children, or simply because of convention. But more and more people are discovering that there are other acceptable and enjoyable options.

on their husbands' sense of responsibility to keep them tied to the relationship even after they were entirely alienated from it. Many marriages are held together by this sense of guilt and responsibility rather than by genuine love and affection. And this holds true even when one person in the marriage deeply loves another person.

All these may be transitional problems that afflict the present adult generation of men and women because they have been brought up with many of the traditional values, such as the ideals of happy and lasting marriages. Some women do not yet realize the high price that must usually be paid for these ideals — aspirations that have to be forgotten, abilities that will never be developed, experiences that are never to be lived, painful compromises that must be made, unhappiness or lack of excitement that is considered a normal part of life. Increasingly, however, as women become aware of the high social and psychological cost of love, marriage, and motherhood on men's terms, they are rebelling; they are becoming more reluctant to commit themselves totally, even to giving and accepting love. Their withdrawal from love into loneliness is very painful since women have been "groomed for love" and without love most women feel that they are outcasts and emotionally dead. In the 1960s many movies portrayed this new reaction of women to love on a man's terms (*Klute, Diary of a Mad Housewife, Thank You All Very Much, The Touch, Sunday, Bloody Sunday,* and *Play It as It Lays*). But this withdrawal may be necessary in order for adult women to become able to redefine themselves independently of a man's love (Haskell, 1973). To become a person in one's own right, independent of others, requires a drastic restructuring of one's significant feelings, roles, preoccupations, and pursuits. Only by a willingness to bear the difficult transitional period can women hope to attain an equal psychological basis with men. In the future, as a result of such a transition (for women as a totality as well as for individual women), it will be possible for women to fit love and its requirements into their lives, rather than suiting and reorienting their lives into a pattern already defined and constructed by the particular man they love as well as by a male-dominated society.

But even when we realize the cost involved in the traditional love marriage and are not willing to pay the price, many of us will not be able to lose the image of the perfect marriage in which husband and wife share the perfect love. Can we and should we share this ideal with our children? Are young people really different? Do they understand love and commitment and marriage differently?

It is true that the rhetoric of some young people in the U.S. glorifies "coolness" and independence. To be "cool" means to love without losing control, without ever clinging to the other person. It means loving yet staying independent, and moreover, giving the person you love his/her independence too. It may mean being able to live apart for long periods of time, allowing for other important relationships and commitments in the life of the one you love. But how can one be passionately in love and stay "cool"? How can one take the risks involved in a "cool" relationship — risks that may cause the relationship to end? How do you cope with feelings of loneliness, rejection, emptiness, unhappiness? Can people be brought up to be able to take life and relationships so lightly, elegantly, joyfully, to enjoy the pleasure of the moment and move from one relationship to another without pain, without anxiety? Can they learn to feel comfortable in multiple relationships with limited or no commitment? What happens then to the meaning of commitment? If the value and strength of legal marital commitment continues to diminish, can we link commitment to love? Can people learn to live with such uncertainty? Can people make genuine commitments in relationships that they cannot expect to last eternally? Do we all perhaps *need* the illusion of "eternal love"? How will our children plan their lives when the illusion of continuity that has been the backbone of the idea of lifelong love and marriage is taken away? Can people live happily without this illusion? Is it not too much stress to plan for a series of loves and commitments (whether legal or not) in one's life? How many people will have the strength and the faith to go on searching for another love and another commitment?

We have been asking too many questions and we are more and more unwilling to accept *musts,* to tell lies, to play tricks and games, and to play-act in order to keep a relationship. On the other hand, we increasingly expect more and more from a love relationship and we want the best of all possible worlds: the love, the warmth, the affection, and a good sexual relationship together with independence, freedom, the ability to be ourselves, to find and develop ourselves, and to grow. And in achieving all this, we want to be honest and open, and to always clearly choose to stay in relationships without doubts, without ambivalence. Maybe we are reaching for the impossible. The perfection in love that we are longing for may be only very short-lived and the pain attached to its end so great that it overshadows the experienced happiness.

Another very serious structural complication is being introduced by the fact that an increasing number of women want to have the opportunity to work in interesting jobs that maximize their abilities and knowledge. Because this is taking place at a period when unemployment is considerable at all occupational levels, it is often very difficult for two people who are married or living together to find jobs in the same location; and it is even more difficult to find the kinds of jobs they want. Many middle- and upper-middle-class couples now live in different cities with a variety of arrangements. What happens to the affective and sexual relationships of such "weekend" or "twice-a-month" couples, especially if this is not merely a temporary pattern? Can passionate love survive this experience or is it only companionate, comfortable "living" relationships that can survive? Is it not to be expected realistically that one of them or both will fall passionately in love with somebody else?

Some people may not want to settle for conventional marriages but also, after having tried, find that they cannot cope with the pain, loneliness, and psychological death felt after the end of a beautiful love relationship. So they may decide to give up their search for the perfect love and settle into a comfortable relationship with someone with whom they can live without great peaks of emotional, sexual, or intellectual enjoyment but also without peaks of anxiety, misery, jealousy, and pain. This type of relationship differs from a conventional marriage because this "comfortable" relationship may often allow both people to do the things that are important to them. Such a relationship may allow partners to help each other grow, find pleasure in each other's company, and even enjoy a warm affection. But we cannot speak here of *love*. This is more of a companionate arrangement between a man and a woman that may involve varying degrees of affection, sexual enjoyment, and intellectual sharing. But perhaps this kind of arrangement doesn't go deep enough. Perhaps the partners will find that they still long for that other kind of love that binds them and tortures them but can also give them the deepest sense of pleasure possible.

Can people grow up not to care for passionate love, not to miss it in their lives and feel perfectly happy in comfortable relationships of different types? Some science fiction stories and movies want us to believe that it is possible, although our biases make us portray them as fascinated by the discovery of passionate love. Do we want our children to be like that, and is it possible that they will change so drastically in the very near future?

What may be very important and helpful for societies such as the American one is the rediscovery of friendship, in which people can have a wide network of close, intimate friends. Changes in men's and women's self-definitions and in the definitions of their relationships can be expected to help the establishment of a greater range of friendships between men and women. With the postponement of marriage and the realization that togetherness and the overemphasis of the couple (before and after marriage) often leads to a dead end, perhaps friendships that continue and survive after marriage and after deep love involvements will become one of our answers. It has been suggested that a brand-new vocabulary may be in order so we can differentiate and describe these new types of relationships. Some of the new terms are: "attaché," referring to a person to whom one has a deep emotional attachment, sexual or asexual; "living friend," referring to a person with whom one shares a household, with or without an emotional or sexual bond (Farrell, 1975); and "intimate friend," referring to a person with whom one has an intensive and extensive bond that endures through time and across the separation of distance (Ramey, 1975). These terms refer to new types of relationships evolving to meet a variety of emotional needs for intimacy and continuity. The existence of a network of a variety of male and female friends is of great importance as a "support system." They will help cushion the pain of the end of a love relationship or a marriage. They will also help people stay more "cool" and independent and less possessive, even when passionate love is involved, since they represent pleasant alternatives. Also, they will diminish the eternal fear and anxiety that faces all of us as we become older.

In addition, even more important, the development of a strong identity, which can endure as we grow and change, can allow us to find a life continuity even as loves, marriages, and different relationships come and go (Kilpatrick, 1975). This implies that both men and women will learn how to stop defining themselves in terms of others; relationships with others will enrich people instead of redefining them, and the severance of relationships will no longer have the power to disintegrate people. To develop such a strong and positive as well as flexible identity is a very difficult achievement for everyone, but even more difficult for women whose "feminine" socialization conditions them to depend on the approval of those around them.

Finally, there is the possibility that in the future people may be able to accept passionate love as a short-lived but precious experience so that husbands and wives, or people who have great affection and a good companionate relationship with each other, reach the point of letting each other be free to experience such relationships. While theoretically this idea is conceivable—some claim that they are already having such a relationship (Francoeur and Francoeur, 1974)—there are unquestionably a number of emotional complications as well as occupational and practical constraints to consider. How can you manage to passionately love someone when you can only see that person occasionally? How is your "permanent" companion to cope with uncertainty, anxiety, jealousy, hurt while you are living your great passion? Can you feel free to love and be as committed as you could or would like to be if you have not severed your relationship with your spouse or companion and you have not made definite emotional, social, and financial commitments? Will not the tendency be to relegate other loves to a secondary level with lesser priority in order not to destroy the secure, comfortable, marital relationship and in order to lessen the stress and strain involved? What will be your relationship with your spouse after the grand passion is over? Will you be able to pick up that involvement without a drastic erosion in the relationship? And what happens when the one spouse continuously falls in love with other people and needs freedom while the other rarely reciprocates and may need more emotional support? What is the meaning of love and commitment in this context? Does commitment mean always coming back to each other between love affairs and the assurance of the existence of an "intimate friend"? Is it not then preferable to openly admit that what some people need is a few "intimate friends" who persist through life, with the freedom to make love commitments to others which may last for varying amounts of time? Why do we need marriage? Provided that all human relationships can become subject to some legal protection and regulations, as is already true in Sweden (Safilios-Rothschild, 1974), perhaps everyone can explore and find the type of mix of love, commitment, sex, security, and continuity that best fits his/her own needs.

Clearly, much of our discussion about the dilemmas of the future is predominantly, if not entirely, relevant to middle- and upper-middle-class people whose economic survival is not at stake and who, therefore, have the luxury of alternatives and options. Working-class and low-income people may be touched differently by these dilemmas and anxieties. Their energies and thoughts must center on the struggle to survive financially—to be able to pay for their housing, their food, and their children's education. Their fears are overshadowed by the great ghost of unemployment and other considerations often seem irrelevant or silly. But we must not assume that the same affective and sexual dilemmas do not touch and shape their lives, even if they may often take a different form. Because limited financial resources negate some options, many compromises have to be made in the type of possible relationships and commitments—but the affective and sexual elements are not necessarily basically different. Furthermore, despite much noise about the fact that the women's movement ideology has not penetrated working-class and low-income women and men, there is in fact considerable evidence that several significant role redefinitions are going on in the occupational and familial roles in this sphere.

Having raised many provocative questions in this book, we could conclude by saying that the dilemmas confronting today's men and women stem from the social and psychological contradictions posed by their needs for some kind of affective continuity and security as well as for change, diversity, and growth. These dilemmas become more complex as more options and alternatives become feasible and acceptable. I do not believe that one model can or should be the *answer*. People need to be flexible, to be able to move from one model to another, and to invent new models along the way. Speculating about how these dilemmas can be handled becomes very difficult because our imaginations and judgments are circumscribed by our experiences and socialization. At present it may be impossible to guess in what ways men and women will feel comfortable in relating to each other once they can feel, think, and act without the excess baggage of masculine-feminine and sexual hangups.

Although it is difficult to determine which of the emerging trends are a stage in the transition and which are with us to stay, some tendencies are consistent and may be indicative of the direction in which intimate human relationships may be moving.

People have a variety of affective and sexual needs, and they increasingly come to recognize that they may need a variety of intimate relationships within which they can be satisfied. In addition, as men and women increasingly move toward social equality, they will want to relate to each other in many different ways. Thus, intimacy between men and women will no longer be based exclusively on sexuality, actual or potential. Other bases—such as friendship, shared experiences, parenthood, intellectual stimulation, or sharing the practical problems of everyday living—will become equally important in and acceptable for the development of intimate relationships. We can foresee a time when some men and women may have a number of intimate relationships, each of which satisfies one or more of their needs. A man and woman may, for example, live together because they find that they are ideal roommates, but both may have other sexual partners and yet other close friends. Love feelings of different types and intensities may exist between this woman and man, as well as between each of them and their different intimate partners. In this way, love between women and men will be able to include a much broader spectrum of feelings, expressions and behaviors beyond sexuality. This extension and diffusion of love into a number of different types of intimate relationships may help diminish people's anxieties about their chances to be loved, as well as their fears of rejection and loneliness.

While it is difficult to predict, it is possible that such future intimate love relationships, freed from holistic, demanding expectations, may have a longer life expectancy than our present love and sexual relationships. But regardless of the degree of permanence in these future relationships, some kind of affective continuity will be ensured, although the basis for intimacy and love may vary from time to time and from relationship to relationship.

As to the extent of exclusivity within each type of intimate relationship, different models with different degrees of exclusivity may co-exist in the future. Some people, always or only sometimes, may need more than one sexual partner, in the same way that they may need more than one close friend, or even more than one partner with whom to have and raise children. Others may, always or only during some stages of their lives, prefer having only one intimate relationship corresponding to each of their major affective and sexual needs. Still others may strive to and be successful in finding only one person with whom to have an all-inclusive love relationship.

I am not predicting that the broadening of the basis for love between women and men will necessarily increase happiness. But it may lead us to a higher level of social organization in which men and women will be able to establish healthy, intimate human relationships and in which all such relationships will be protected by humanitarian controls and mutual responsibilities. And it may help us evolve to a level at which we can cope and within which we can experience and express our feelings and emotions with less alienation.

References

Abstract of Protocol on Justice Department Matters Held Before the King in Council, Safiero, Sweden, August 15, 1969 (mimeographed).

ACKER, JOAN, and DONALD P. VAN HOUTEN, "Differential Recruitment and Control: The Sex Structuring of Organizations," *Administrative Science Quarterly*, 19, no. 2 (1974), 211-20.

ARONSON, ELLIOT, and VERA ARONSON, "Does a Woman's Attractiveness Influence Men's Nonsexual Reactions?" *Medical Aspects of Human Sexuality*, 5, no. 11 (1971), 12, 17, 20, 21, 25-27.

BACH, GEORGE R., and HERB GOLDBERG, *Creative Aggression.* New York: Avon Books, 1975.

BALSWICK, JACK O., and CHARLES W. PEEK, "The Inexpressive Male and Family Relationships During Early Adulthood," *Sociological Symposium*, 4 (Spring 1970), 1-12.

BALSWICK, JACK O., and JAMES LINCOLN COLLIER, "Why Husbands Can't Say 'I Love You,' " *Woman's Day*, 37(April 1974), 66, 158, and 160.

BART, PAULINE B., "Why Women's Status Changes in Middle Age: The Turns of the Social Ferris Wheel," *Sociological Symposium,* Vol. 3, 1969, pp. 1-18.

BARTELL, GILBERT D., *Group Sex.* New York: Signet Books, 1971.

BELL, DANIEL, "Welcome to the Post-Industrial Society," *Physics Today* (February 1976), 46-47.

BELL, ROBERT R., *Marriage and Family Interaction* (3rd ed.), pp. 112-22. Homewood, Ill.: Dorsey, 1971.

BELL, ROBERT R., "Sexuality and Sex Roles," paper prepared for the Working Conference to Develop Teaching Materials on Family and Sex Roles, Detroit, Michigan, November 10-12, 1975.

BENGIS, INGRID, "What We Do Not Say Is That We Are All, Every Last One of Us, Scared of Love's Power to Create and Destroy," *Ms.,* vol. 1, no. 5 (November 1972), pp. 64-67, 122, 125-27.

BENSON, LEONARD, *The Family Bond. Marriage, Love, and Sex in America,* pp. 115-16. New York: Random House, 1971.

BERNARD, JESSIE, "Infidelity: Some Moral and Social Issues," in Jules H. Masserman (Ed.), *The Psychodynamics of Work and Marriage,* Vol. XVI. New York: Grune and Stratton, Inc., 1970, pp. 99-126.

BLUMSTEIN, PHILIP W., and PEPPER SCHWARTZ, "Bisexual Woman," in Jacqueline P. Wiseman (Ed.), *The Social Psychology of Sex,* pp. 154-62. New York: Harper & Row, 1976, pp. 154-62.

BOSQUET, MICHAEL, "Quand la médecine rend malade," *Le Nouvel Observateur* (October 21, 1974), 84-85, 88, 93, 104, 109, 112, 118.

BOYLAN, BRIAN RICHARD, *Infidelity.* Englewood Cliffs, N.J.: Prentice-Hall, 1971.

BRADLEY, NADIA, "La scandale de la virginité," *Lamatif,* 25 (December 1968), 15-17.

BRODERICK, CARLFRED B., and MARY W. HICKS, "Zu Einer Typologie von Verhaltensmustern bei der Brautwerbung in den USA," (Toward a Typology of American Courtship Patterns), in Günther Luschen and Eugen Lupri (Eds.), *Soziologie der Familie,* pp. 473-89. Westdeutscher Verlag Opladen, 1970.

CHAFETZ, JANET SALTZMAN, *Masculine/Feminine or Human?* Itasca, Ill.: F. E. Peacock, 1974.

CHAN, LILY MARY VERONICA, "Foot Binding in Chinese Women and its Psycho-Social Implications," *Canadian Psychiatric Association Journal*, 15, no. 2 (1970), 229-31.

CHARLTON, LINDA, "Navy Wives Irate at Idea of Women on Warships," *The New York Times*, August 27, 1972.

COLEMAN, JAMES S., "Female Status and Premarital Sexual Codes," *American Journal of Sociology*, 72 (March 1966), 217.

COLLINS, RANDALL, *Conflict Sociology. Toward an Explanatory Science*. New York: Academic Press, 1975.

COMBS, ROBERT H., and WILLIAM F. KENKEL, "Sex Differences in Dating Aspirations and Satisfaction with Computer-Selected Partners," *Journal of Marriage and the Family*, 28, no. 1 (1966), 62-66.

CUBER, JOHN F., and PEGGY B. HARROFF, *Sex and the Significant Americans*. Baltimore: Penguin Books, 1968.

DAVIS, MURRAY S., *Intimate Relations*. New York: The Free Press, 1973.

FABIAN, JUDITH J., "The Role of the Therapist in the Process of Sexual Emancipation," *Psychiatric Opinion*, 10, no. 4 (1973), 31-33.

FARRELL, WARREN, *The Liberated Man*. New York: Bantam Books, 1975.

"Female Pleasure Patterns," *Human Behavior*, Vol. 4 (October 1975), 60-61.

FIRESTONE, SHULAMITH, *The Dialectic of Sex*. New York: William Morrow & Co., 1970.

FOX, GREER LITTON, "Before Marriage: An Assessment of Organization and Change in the Premarital Period," paper prepared for The Working Conference to Develop Teaching Materials on Family and Sex Roles, November 10-12, 1975, Detroit, Michigan.

FRANCOEUR, ANNA K., and ROBERT T. FRANCOEUR, *Hot and Cool Sex: Cultures in Conflict*. New York: Harcourt Brace Jovanovich, 1974.

GINSBERG, GEORGE, WILLIAM FROSCH, and THEODORE SHAPIRO, "The New Impotence," *Archives of General Psychiatry*, 26 (March 1972), 218-22.

GLICK, PAUL C., "A Demographer Looks at American Families," *Journal of Marriage and the Family,* Vol. 31, no. 1 (February, 1975), pp. 15-26.

GOLDBERG, HERB, *"The Hazards of Being Male,"* Plainview, N.Y.: Nash Publishing Co., 1976.

GREER, GERMAINE, *The Female Eunuch.* New York: McGraw-Hill, 1971.

GUBBAY, MICHELLE, "The Paradise Lounge: Working as a Cocktail Waitress in a Strip Club," in Rosalyn Baxandall, Linda Gordon, and Susan Reverby (Eds.), *Women Working.* New York: Random House, 1976.

———, "Women and Men: A Study of the Paradise Lounge," unpublished manuscript, 1973.

HARRELL, W. ANDREW, and JUNE SAGAN, "Sex Differences in the Perception of Rape and the Sentencing of Rapists," paper presented at the American Sociological Association meetings, Montreal, Canada, August 1974.

HASKELL, MOLLY, *From Reverence to Rape: The Treatment of Women in the Movies.* Baltimore: Penguin Books, 1973.

HELD, JEAN FRANCIS, "Les matamores du sexe," *Réalités* (October 1975), 54-57.

HENLEY, NANCY M., "The Politics of Touch," paper presented at the American Psychological Association meetings, Miami Beach, Florida, September 1970.

———, "Power, Sex, and Nonverbal Communication," *Berkeley Journal of Sociology,* 18 (1973-74), 1-26.

HOCHSCHILD, ARLIE R., "Attending to, Codifying and Managing Feelings: Sex Differences in Love," paper presented at the American Sociological Association meetings, August 1975, San Francisco.

———, personal communication in the form of comments on the book, Berkeley, California, June 5, 1976.

HUANG, LUCY JEN, "Research with Unmarried Cohabiting Couples: Including Non-Exclusive Sexual Relations," Illinois State University, 1974, unpublished manuscript.

ISRAEL, JOACHIM, and ROSMARI ELIASSON, "Consumption Society, Sex Roles and Sexual Behavior," *Acta Sociologica* 14, nos. 1, 2, (1971), 68-82.

JONES, CATHALEENE, and ELLIOT ARONSON, "Attribution of Fault to a Rape Victim as a Function of Respectability of the Victim," *Journal of Personality and Social Psychology*, 26, no. 3 (1973), 415-19.

KANIN, EUGENE J., KAREN D. DAVIDSON, and SONIA R. SCHECK, "A Research Note on Male-Female Differentials in the Experience of Heterosexual Love," *The Journal of Sex Research*, 6, no. 1 (February 1970), 64-72.

KASTEN, KATHERINE, "Toward a Psychology of Being: A Masculine Mystique," *Journal of Humanistic Psychology*, 12, no. 2 (Fall 1972), 23-43.

KATZ, JUDITH MILSTEIN, "How Do You Love Me? Let me Count the Ways (The Phenomenology of Being Loved)," *Sociological Inquiry*, 46, no. 1 (1976), 17-22.

KEPHART, WILLIAM M., "Some Correlates of Romantic Love," *Journal of Marriage and the Family*, 29, no. 3 (1967), 470-74.

KILPATRICK, WILLIAM, *Identity and Intimacy.* New York: Dell, 1975.

KOMAROVSKY, MIRRA, *Dilemmas of Masculinity. A Study of College Youth.* New York: W. W. Norton, 1976.

KOOY, GERRIT A., "A De-Mythologizing of the Erotique in the West," Wageningen, Holland: Department of Rural Sociology, Spring 1969, unpublished manuscript.

LAWS, JUDITH LONG, "Toward a Model of Female Sexual Identity," *Midway* (Summer 1970), 39-75.

LIPMAN-BLUMEN, JEAN, "Preliminary Thoughts on Reconceptualizing the Area of Family Structure," paper prepared for the Merrill-Palmer Conference on Reconceptualizing Family Sociology in the Light of Sex Role Research, Detroit, Michigan, November 1975.

————, "Toward a Homosocial Theory of Sex Roles: An Explanation of the Social Institutions of Sex Segregation," *Signs*, 1, no. 3, Part 2 (Spring 1976), 15-31.

LYONS, RICHARD D., "Sex Called Problem in Half of Marriages," *The New York Times*, June 19, 1972.

MANN, JAY, and HARVEY CAPLAN, "Toward a Reconceptualization of Sexuality," paper commissioned by the Advisory Council of the Project on Human Sexual Development, Cambridge, Mass., November 1975.

MARCIANO, TERESA DONATI, "The Unmarriageability of Educated Women," paper presented at the International Workshop on Marriage and the Family, Dubrovnik, Yugoslavia, June 1975.

MASTERS, WILLIAM, and VIRGINIA E. JOHNSON, *The Pleasure Bond.* New York: Bantam Books, 1975.

MAYNARD, JOYCE, "The Liberation of Total Woman," *The New York Times Magazine* (September 28, 1975), 9-66.

MERNISSI, FATIMA, *The Effects of Modernization of the Male-Female Dynamics in a Muslim Society: Morocco.* Ann Arbor, Michigan: University Microfilms, 1973.

———, *Beyond the Veil, Male-Female Dynamics in a Modern Muslim Society.* Cambridge, Mass.: Shenkman, 1975.

MILLER, JEAN BAKER, "Sexual Inequality: Men's Dilemma," *American Journal of Psychoanalysis,* Vol. 32, no. 2 (1972), 147-55.

MILLUM, TREVOR, *Images of Women: Advertising in Women's Magazines.* London: Chatts & Windus, 1975.

MORELL, CAROLYN, "Love and Will: A Feminist Critique," *Journal of Humanistic Psychology,* 13, no. 2 (Spring 1973), 35-46.

MULLIGAN, LINDA W., "Wives, Women and Wife Role Behavior: An Alternative Cross-Cultural Perspective," *International Journal of Comparative Sociology,* 13, no. 1 (March 1972), 36-47.

MYER, LONNY, and HUNTER LIGGITT, "A New View on Adultery," *Sexual Behavior* (February 1972), 52-62.

NORTON, ARTHUR J., and PAUL C. GLICK, "Marital Instability: Past, Present, and Future," *Journal of Social Issues,* Vol. 32, no. 1 (1976), 5-20.

O'NEILL, NENA, and GEORGE O'NEILL, *Open Marriage.* New York: Avon Books, 1972.

PAINE, ROBERT, "In Search of Friendship: An Exploratory Analysis in Middle Class Culture," *Man,* 4 (December 1969), 505-24.

PALEOLOGOS, PAUL, *The Woman According to Greek Patterns.* Athens: Asteri Publishers, 1975.

PANKIN, ROBERT M., "The Romantic Myth, Sexism and the Bureaucratic Property System," paper presented at the annual meetings of the North Central Sociological Association, Cincinnati, Ohio, May 1973.

PARCA, GABRIELLA, *Les Italiens et l'Amour.* Paris: Gallimard, 1968.

PASCON, P., and M. BENTAHAR, "Ce que disent 296 Jeunes Ruraux," *Bulletin Economique et Social du Maroc,* 32 (Janvier-Juin 1969), 112-13.

Patterns of Sex and Love: A Study of French Women and Their Morals. New York: Crown, 1961.

PETERSON, JAMES A. "The Office Wife," *Sexual Behavior,* 1, no. 5 (August 1971), 3-10.

POGREBIN, LETTIE COTTIN, "8 Hours a Day, 5 Days a Week, 50 Weeks a Year: The Intimate Politics of Working with Men," *Ms,* 4, no. 4 (1975), 48-51, 105,106.

Policewomen on Patrol, Major Findings: First Report, Vol. I. A Police Foundation paper. Washington, D.C.: Police Foundation, February 1973.

PRATHER, JANE, "Why Can't Women Be More Like Men? A Summary of the Sociopsychological Factors Hindering Women's Advancement in the Professions," *American Behavioral Scientist,* 15, no. 2 (November-December 1971), 172-82.

RAJOGOPALAN, C., "Social Change: An Analysis of Role Conflict and Deviation," *Indian Journal of Social Work,* 24, no. 1 (April 1963), 11-18.

RAMEY, J. W., *Intimate Relationships.* Englewood Cliffs, N.J.: Prentice-Hall, 1976.

RAPOPORT, RHONA, and RAPOPORT, ROBERT, *Dual Career Families.* Harmondsworth, Middlesex, England: Penguin Books Ltd., 1971.

RODGERS, JOANN, "Rush to Surgery," *The New York Times Magazine,* (September 21, 1975), 34-42.

ROSENFELD, ALBERT, "Science, Sex, and Tomorrow's Morality," in Frank D. Cox (Ed.), *American Marriage: A Changing Scene?* pp. 3-15. Dubuque, Iowa: William C. Brown, 1972.

RUBIN, ZICK, "Lovers and Other Strangers: The Development of Intimacy in Encounters and Relationships," *American Scientist,* 62 (March-April 1974), 182-90.

SAFILIOS-ROTHSCHILD, CONSTANTINA, "Morality, Courtship and Love in Greek Folklore," *Southern Folklore Quarterly*, 29, no. 4 (December 1965), 297-308.

_____, " 'Good' and 'Bad' Girls in Modern Greek Movies," *The Journal of Marriage and the Family*, 30, no. 3 (1968), 527-31.

_____, "Honor Crimes in Contemporary Greece," *The British Journal of Sociology*, 2, no. 2 (June 1969), 205-18.

_____, "A Cross-Cultural Study of Women's Marital, Educational and Occupational Options," *Acta Sociologica*, 14, nos. 1, 2 (1971), 96-113.

_____, *Toward a Sociology of Women*. New York: Wiley & Sons, 1972.

_____, *Women and Social Policy*. Englewood Cliffs, N.J.: Prentice-Hall, 1974.

_____, "The Current Status of Women Cross-Culturally: Changes and Persisting Barriers," *Theological Studies*, Special Issue on Women, 36, no. 4 (December 1975), 577-604. (a)

_____. "Sex Role Socialization Patterns in Selected Societies," *Educational Testing Service Research Bulletin*, **RB**-75-39 (December 1975). (b)

_____, "A Macro- and Micro-Examination of Family Power and Love: An Exchange Model," *Journal of Marriage and the Family*, 38, no. 2 (1976). (b)

_____, "Dual Linkages Between the Occupational and Family System: A Macrosociological Analysis," *Signs*, Vol. 1, no. 3, part 2 (Spring 1976). (a)

_____, *The Modern Greek Family: I. Family Dynamics*. Athens: The National Center for Social Research, 1977. (a)

_____, "Sexuality, Power, and Freedom," in Lilian Troll, Joan Israel and Kenneth Israel, 1977.(a) *The Older Woman*. Englewood Cliffs, N.J.: Prentice-Hall, 1977 (in press). (b)

SEIDENBERG. ROBERT, *Marriage in Life and Literature*. New York: Philosophical Library, 1970.

_____, "Is Sex Without Sexism Possible?" *Sexual Behavior*, 2, no. 1 (January 1972), 47-62.

SHEEHY, GAIL, "The Sexual Diamond: Facing the Facts of the Human Sexual Life Cycles," *New York* (January 26, 1976), 28-39.

SIGALL, HAROLD, and DAVID LANDY, "Radiating Beauty: Effects of Having a Physically Attractive Partner on Person Perception," *Journal of Personality and Social Psychology,* 28, no. 2 (1973), 218-24.

SMITH, RICHARD W., "Covert Discrimination Against Women as Colleagues," paper read at the American Psychological Association meetings, Honolulu, September 1972.

STANNARD, UNA, "The Mask of Beauty," in Vivian Gornick and Barbara K. Moran (Eds.), *Women in Sexist Society,* pp. 187-203. New York: New American Library, 1971.

STORA-SANDOR, JUDITH, *Alexandra Kollontai: Marxisme et revolution sexuelle.* Paris: François Maspéro, 1973.

SULLEROT, EVELYNE, *Droit de regard.* Paris: Denoel/Gonthier, 1970.

VALABRÈGUE, CATHERINE, *La condition masculine.* Paris: Petite Bibliothèque Payot, 1968.

WALSHOK, MARY LINDENSTEIN, "Sex Role Typing and Feminine Sexuality," paper presented at the American Sociological Association meetings, New York City, August 1973.

WALSTER, ELAINE, "Passionate Love," in Arlene Skolnick and Jerome H. Skolnick (Eds.). *Intimacy, Family, and Society.* Boston: Little, Brown, 1974.

WALSTER, ELAINE G., WILLIAM WALSTER, JANE PILAVIN, and LYNN SCHMIDT, " 'Playing Hard to Get': Understanding an Elusive Phenomenon," *Journal of Personality and Social Psychology,* 26, no. 1 (1973), 113-21.

WILKINSON, MELVIN, "Romantic Love: The Great Equalizer? Sexism in Popular Music," *The Family Coordinator,* 25, no. 2 (1976), 161-66.

WISEMAN, JACQUELINE P., "The Search for Sexual Pleasure," in Jacqueline P. Wiseman (Ed.), *The Social Psychology of Sex,* pp. 181-92. New York: Harper & Row, 1976 pp. 181-92.

ZETTERBERG, HANS L., "The Secret Ranking," *Journal of Marriage and the Family,* 28, no. 2 (1966), 134-42.

ZISKIN, JAY, and MAE ZISKIN, *The Extra-Marital Contract.* Los Angeles: Nash Publishing Co., 1973

Index

Abortion, 33
Affectionate love, 7, 10
Alchemy of love, 11, 12-13
Attractiveness, 18, 27-28, 35-39, 92

"Bad" women, 30, 48, 50, 55-56, 57, 62, 120, 124-25
Bangladesh, 27
Bestiality, 57
Birth control, 4, 33
Brother-sister love, 11

Career women, 4, 15, 86-93, 132
Chinese women, 37

Dehumanization of love, 54-65, 126
Dependency, 12, 32, 63
Desirability, 13
Divorce, 20, 27, 102-3, 106, 129
Double standard, sexual, 42-43, 59, 111, 116, 117, 124
Dowry, 34

Egypt, 37
Eternal love, 67-68
Extramarital sexual relations, 69-70, 77-78, 91

Fashion, 36-38
Femininity, 1, 22-25, 121
    definition of, 63
    incompatibility of love and, 63-65
Femmes fatales, 50, 62
Fidelity, 69-70
Friendships, 11, 80-81, 94-98, 103
Frigidity, 113, 121

Greece, 18, 50, 57, 75, 94

Homosexuality, 57, 73-74, 80-81, 104
Honor crimes, 34-35
Hysterectomy, 33

Impotence, 107, 113-14, 121
India, 88
Indifference, 13
Intelligence, 31
"Intimate friend," 134, 135
Italy, 20, 24, 57

Kidnapping, 75

Life expectancy, 21
"Living friend," 134
Loneliness, 12, 130
Love
    affectionate, 7, 10
    alchemy of, 11, 12-13
    dehumanization of, 54-65, 126
    elements of, 6
    end of, 8, 10
    eternal, 67-68
    fear of, 16, 61
    femininity, incompatibility with, 63-65
    fidelity, 69-70
    future for, 116-38
    humanization of, 126-28
    love-adventure, 6, 7, 64
    love-friendship, 6, 7
    marriage and, 16-21
    masculinity, incompatibility with, 60-63
    mature, 3, 7, 10-11, 15-16, 40
    myths about, 65-70
    obstacles to development of, 54-79
    passionate, 7-8, 13, 19, 129, 132-35

Love (cont.)
  redefinition, need for, 21
  romantic, 3, 8-9, 13, 65-67
  sexuality and, 21-25, 55-58
  social inequality and, 70-79
  true, 8-9
  variety of, 5-6
Love-adventure, 6, 7, 64
Love courts, 16
Love-friendship, 6, 7

Marriage, 66-67
  affectionate love in, 10
  buying brides, 33-34
  eternal love and, 67-68
  fidelity, 69-70
  love and, 16-21
  open, 70
  redefinition, need for, 21
  togetherness, 68-69
  transitional period and, 99-107
  two-career, 15
Masculinity, 1, 22-25, 53, 56, 71-72, 121, 124
  incompatibility of love and, 60-63
Masturbation, 57
Mature love, 3, 7, 10-11, 15-16, 40
Men
  attractiveness, 38
  divorce, 106
  fashion, 37, 38
  friendships, nonromantic, 94-98
  lack of mutual trust, 58-60
  objectification of, 41-53
  objectification of women, 26-40
  remarriage, 106
  sexual performance, 107-15, 123-25
  socialization, 51, 104, 105
  strangers, encounters with, 82-86
  success objects, 38
  treated as children, 50-53
  work relationships, 86-93
  see also Love; Marriage; Sexuality
Men's liberation movement, 104
Mistresses, 77-78
Morocco, 57
Mother-child love, 11
Mother image, 51
Muslim societies, 61

Occupational sex segregation, 86-89
Open marriage, 70
Orgasm, 108, 110, 119, 123

Pakistan, 87
Parea, 94
Parenthood, 79
Passionate love, 7-8, 13, 19, 129, 132-35
Possessiveness, 63, 100
Premarital sexual relations, 27, 55
Prostitution, 48, 57, 77, 91

Rape, 27, 29, 32, 46, 56, 75
Rejection, 13
Remarriage, 103, 106
Reputation, 46
Romantic love, 3, 8-9, 13, 65-67

Saudi Arabia, 32

Sex-role stereotypes, 3, 22, 42-43, 57, 59, 60, 62, 64, 65
  71, 77-79, 95, 96, 108, 120, 121, 123, 124
Sexual double standard, 42-43, 59, 111, 116, 117, 124
Sexual drives, 107-12
Sexual exploitation, 87-88
Sexuality
  as commodity, 3, 47-50
  dehumanization of, 54-65, 126
  future for, 116-38
  humanization of, 126-28
  love and, 21-25, 55-58
  reconceptualization of, 123-26
  sexual teasing, 3, 43-47, 64
Sexual performance, 107-15, 123-25
Sexual teasing, 3, 43-47, 64
Sicily, 75
Social change, 99-107
Social differentiation, 1-2
Social inequality, 1, 2, 70-79
Socialization process
  of men, 51, 104, 105
  of women, 39, 43, 55, 56, 121, 134
Social mobility, 1, 2
Social status, 17, 18
Sodomy, 57
Strangers, encounters with, 82-86
Sweden, 66-67, 135
Swinging couples, 70, 109

Teasing, sexual, 3, 43-47, 64
Togetherness, 68-69
Total Woman workshops, 39
Touching, 32
True love, 8-9

Virginity, 24, 27, 77, 111, 113, 117, 127

Women
  abortion, 33
  attractiveness, 27-28, 35-37, 39, 92
  "bad," 30, 48, 50, 55-56, 57, 62, 120, 124-25
  birth control, 4, 33
  divorce, 102-3
  early "liberated," 14
  friendships, nonromantic, 94-98
  frigidity, 113, 121
  inequality, 70-79
  intelligence, 31
  lack of mutual trust, 58-60
  mother image, 51
  objectification of, 26-40
  objectification of men, 41-53
  option to pursue men, 119-22
  orgasm, 108, 110, 119, 123
  remarriage, 103
  self-evaluation, 35-40
  sexuality of older, 98
  sexual performance, 107-15, 123-25
  sexual teasing, 3, 43-47, 64
  socialization, 39, 43, 55, 56, 121, 134
  strangers, encounters with, 82-86
  treatment of men as children, 50-53
  value of, 26-35
  work relationships, 86-93
  see also Love; Marriage; Sexuality
Women's liberation movement, 4, 104
Work relationships, 4, 86-93, 132

Youth, 100, 131